144 Arthritis-Preventive Juice, Salad, and Meal Recipes:

The Necessary Cookbook to Naturally Reducing Aches and Pains

By

Joe Correa CSN

COPYRIGHT

© 2019 Live Stronger Faster Inc.

All rights reserved

Reproduction or translation of any part of this work beyond that permitted by section 107 or 108 of the 1976 United States Copyright Act without the permission of the copyright owner is unlawful.

This publication is designed to provide accurate and authoritative information in regard to the subject matter covered. It is sold with the understanding that neither the author nor the publisher is engaged in rendering medical advice. If medical advice or assistance is needed, consult with a doctor. This book is considered a guide and should not be used in any way detrimental to your health. Consult with a physician before starting this nutritional plan to make sure it's right for you.

ACKNOWLEDGEMENTS

This book is dedicated to my friends and family that have had mild or serious illnesses so that you may find a solution and make the necessary changes in your life.

144 Arthritis-Preventive Juice, Salad, and Meal Recipes:

The Necessary Cookbook to Naturally Reducing Aches and Pains

By

Joe Correa CSN

CONTENTS

Copyright

Acknowledgements

About The Author

Introduction

Commitment

144 Arthritis-Preventive Juice, Salad, and Meal Recipes: The Necessary Cookbook to Naturally Reducing Aches and Pains

Additional Titles from This Author

ABOUT THE AUTHOR

After years of Research, I honestly believe in the positive effects that proper nutrition can have over the body and mind. My knowledge and experience has helped me live healthier throughout the years and which I have shared with family and friends. The more you know about eating and drinking healthier, the sooner you will want to change your life and eating habits.

Nutrition is a key part in the process of being healthy and living longer so get started today. The first step is the most important and the most significant.

INTRODUCTION

144 Arthritis-Preventive Juice, Salad, and Meal Recipes: The Necessary Cookbook to Naturally Reducing Aches and Pains

By Joe Correa CSN

A proper nutrition plays an important role in reducing the risk of arthritis. Our modern diet, based on animal-derived foods, refined sugar, and foods that provoke the immune system response increases the sensitivity for inflammation which leads to this painful disease. With a good nutrition, consistency, and good lifestyle choices, your health will improve significantly and your body will get a chance to resist the inflammation. Furthermore, healthy, fresh, and unprocessed foods will reduce the risk of obesity which not only contributes to the onset and progress of arthritis but also makes your joints carry more weight. Excess weight directly damages your joints and contributes to both - development and progress of this disease.

The main reason I have created this great collection of arthritis preventing recipes was to give you a quick and simple way to get all the nutrients you need in order to boost your immune system, cleanse your body, and lose some weight all at the same time. Juicing is one of the best ways to nourish your body with amazingly valuable antioxidants and other important substances in just a few minutes. This collection of recipes is especially practical for people with busy schedules who have very little to prepare everything. It's also a perfect option for those of you who don't enjoy eating specific fruits or vegetables throughout the day, but still want to get huge amounts of vitamins and minerals into their body.

I hope these powerful recipes will serve as a guide for your arthritis problems. These juices, salads, and meals will make your digestion easier and will help eliminate dangerous toxins that lead to inflammation and arthritis. This book is all about getting the right nutrients you need in a more convenient way and preventing arthritis once and for all.

COMMITMENT

In order to improve my condition, I *(your name)*, commit to eating more of these foods on a daily basis and to exercise at least 30 minutes daily:

- Berries (especially blueberries), peaches, cherries, apples, apricots, oranges, lemon juice, grapefruit, tangerines, mandarins, pears, etc.
- Broccoli, spinach, collard greens, sweet potatoes, avocado, artichoke, baby corn, carrots, celery, cauliflower, onions, etc.
- Whole grains, steel-cut oats, oatmeal, quinoa, barley, etc.
- Black beans, red bean beans, garbanzo beans, lentils, etc.
- Nuts and seeds including: walnuts, cashews, flaxseeds, sesame seeds, etc.
- Fish
- 8 – 10 glasses of water

Sign here

X_____

144 ARTHRITIS-PREVENTIVE JUICE, SALAD, AND MEAL RECIPES: THE NECESSARY COOKBOOK TO NATURALLY REDUCING ACHES AND PAINS

JUICE RECIPES

1. **Cherry Cucumber Juice**

Ingredients:

2 cups of fresh cherries, pitted

1 large cucumber, sliced

1 large lemon, peeled

1 medium-sized Granny smith apple, cored

2 oz of water

Preparation:

Using a colander, wash the cherries under cold running water. Cut in half and remove the pits. Set aside.

Wash the cucumber and cut into thick slices. Set aside.

Peel the lemon and cut lengthwise in half. Set aside.

Wash the apple and remove the core. Cut into bite-sized pieces and set aside.

Now, combine cherries, cucumber, lemon, and apple in a juicer and process until juiced. Transfer to serving glasses and stir in the water. Add few ice cubes before serving.

Enjoy!

Nutritional information per serving: Kcal: 296, Protein: 6.6g, Carbs: 88.4g, Fats: 1.4g

2. Orange Apricot Juice

Ingredients:

2 large oranges, peeled

2 large apricots, pitted

1 cup of pomegranate seeds

1 cup of green grapes

1 large lemon, peeled

1 small ginger slice, peeled

Preparation:

Peel the oranges and divide into wedges. Set aside.

Wash the apricots and cut in half. Remove the pits and cut into small pieces. Set aside.

Cut the top of the pomegranate fruit using a sharp knife. Slice down to each of the white membranes inside of the fruit. Pop the seeds into a measuring cup and set aside.

Peel the lemon and cut lengthwise in half. Set aside.

Peel the ginger slice and set aside.

Now, combine oranges, apricots, pomegranate, lemon, and

ginger in a juicer. Process until well juiced and transfer to serving glasses. Refrigerate for 20 minutes before serving.

Nutritional information per serving: Kcal: 294, Protein: 7.2g, Carbs: 88.9g, Fats: 2.3g

3. Blueberry Mint Juice

Ingredients:

1 cup of blueberries

1 cup of fresh mint, torn

1 large red apple, cored

1 large cucumber, sliced

2 oz of coconut water

Preparation:

Place the blueberries in a colander and wash under cold running water. Drain and set aside.

Wash the mint thoroughly and torn with hands. Set aside.

Wash the apple and cut in half. Remove the core and cut into bite-sized pieces. Set aside.

Wash the cucumber and gently peel it. Cut into thin slices and set aside.

Now, combine blueberries, mint, apple, and cucumber in a juicer. Process until juiced and transfer to serving glasses. Stir in the coconut water and refrigerate for 15 minutes, or add some ice before serving.

Enjoy!

Nutritional information per serving: Kcal: 258, Protein: 4.7g, Carbs: 74.6g, Fats: 1.6g

4. Strawberry Mango Juice

Ingredients:

6 large strawberries, chopped

1 cup of mango, peeled and chopped

1 cup of cantaloupe, chopped

1 large cucumber, sliced

2 oz of coconut water

Preparation:

Wash the strawberries and cut into bite-sized pieces. Set aside.

Peel the mango and cut into small chunks. Fill the measuring cup and reserve the rest for later.

Cut the cantaloupe in half and scoop out the seeds. Cut two wedges and peel them. Chop into chunks and fill the measuring cup. Reserve the rest of the cantaloupe in a refrigerator.

Wash the cucumber and cut into thick slices. Set aside.

Now, combine strawberries, mango, cantaloupe, and cucumber in a juicer and process until juiced. Transfer to serving glasses and stir in the coconut water. Refrigerate for 30 minutes before serving.

Enjoy!

Nutritional information per serving: Kcal: 209, Protein: 5.3g, Carbs: 56.6g, Fats: 1.5g

5.   Avocado Citrus Juice

Ingredients:

1 cup of avocado, pitted and chopped

1 large cucumber, sliced

1 large lemon, peeled

1 cup of fresh spinach, torn

1 large lime, peeled

1 small ginger knob, peeled

3 oz of water

Preparation:

Peel the avocado and cut in half. Remove the pit and chop into chunks. Set aside.

Wash the cucumber and cut into thick slices. Set aside.

Peel the lemon and lime. Cut lengthwise in half and set aside.

Wash the spinach thoroughly and torn with hands. Set aside.

Peel the ginger knob and set aside.

Now, combine avocado, cucumber, lemon, lime, spinach, and ginger in a juicer. Process until juiced and transfer to serving glasses. Stir in the water and refrigerate for 20 minutes before serving.

Enjoy!

Nutritional information per serving: Kcal: 269, Protein: 6.7g, Carbs: 35g, Fats: 22.6g

6. Artichoke Turmeric Juice

Ingredients:

1 large artichoke, peeled and chopped

1 cup of Brussels sprouts, trimmed

1 large carrot, sliced

1 cup of fresh celery, chopped

1 cup of turnip greens, chopped

1 large green apple, cored

½ tsp of turmeric, ground

2 oz of water

Preparation:

Using a sharp knife, trim off the outer leaves of the artichoke. Cut into small pieces and set aside.

Trim off the outer leaves of the Brussels sprouts and wash them thoroughly. Cut in half and set aside.

Wash the carrot and cut into thin slices. Set aside.

Wash the celery and chop it into bite-sized pieces. Set aside.

Wash the apple and cut in half. Remove the core and cut into bite-sized pieces. Set aside.

Wash the turnip greens thoroughly and torn with hands. Set aside.

Now, combine artichoke, Brussels sprouts, carrot, celery, turnip greens, and apple in a juicer. Process until well juiced and transfer to serving glasses. Stir in the turmeric and water. Add some ice before serving.

Nutritional information per serving: Kcal: 205, Protein: 11.3g, Carbs: 66.7g, Fats: 1.4g

7. Watermelon Orange Juice

Ingredients:

2 cups of watermelon, chopped

1 large orange, peeled

1 cup of raspberries

1 large kiwi, peeled

2 oz coconut water

Preparation:

Cut the watermelon lengthwise. For 2 cups, you will need about 2 large wedges. Peel and cut into chunks. Remove the seeds and set aside. Reserve the rest of the melon for some other juices. Set aside.

Peel the orange and divide into wedges. Set aside.

Wash the raspberries thoroughly under cold running water. Drain and set aside.

Peel the kiwi and cut lengthwise in half. Set aside.

Now, combine watermelon, orange, raspberries, and kiwi in a juicer. Process until juiced and transfer to serving glasses. Stir in the coconut water and refrigerate for 15

minutes before serving.

Nutritional information per serving: Kcal: 232, Protein: 5.8g, Carbs: 71.4g, Fats: 1.8g

8. Salted Beet Tomato Juice

Ingredients:

2 cups of beets, trimmed

1 large Roma tomato, chopped

1 large cucumber, sliced

3 large radishes, trimmed

½ tsp of fresh rosemary, chopped

¼ tsp of sea salt

1 oz of water

Preparation:

Wash the beets and trim off the green parts. Cut into small pieces and set aside.

Wash the tomato and place it in a bowl. Cut into bite-sized pieces and reserve the tomato juice while cutting. Set aside.

Wash the cucumber and cut into thin slices. Set aside.

Wash the radishes and trim off the green ends. Cut in half and set aside.

Now, combine beets, tomato, cucumber, radishes, and rosemary in a juicer. Process until well juiced and transfer to serving glasses. Stir in the salt and water. Refrigerate for 10 minutes before serving.

Enjoy!

Nutritional information per serving: Kcal: 152, Protein: 8.2g, Carbs: 44.9g, Fats: 1.2g

9. Pepper Squash Juice

Ingredients:

3 large red bell peppers, chopped

1 cup of butternut squash, cubed

1 cup of parsnip, sliced

1 tbsp of fresh parsley, chopped

2 oz of water

Preparation:

Wash the red bell peppers and cut lengthwise in half. Remove the seeds and chop into small pieces.

Peel the butternut squash and remove the seeds using a spoon. Cut into small cubes and fill the measuring cup. Reserve the rest of the squash for some other recipe. Wrap in a plastic foil and refrigerate.

Wash the parsnip and peel it. Cut into thin slices and set aside.

Now, combine bell peppers, butternut squash, parsnip, and parsley in a juicer. Process until well juiced and transfer to serving glasses. Stir in the water and add some ice.

Serve immediately.

Nutritional information per serving: Kcal: 238, Protein: 7.9g, Carbs: 70.2g, Fats: 2.1g

10. Papaya Pomegranate Juice

Ingredients:

1 large papaya, peeled and chopped

1 cup of pomegranate seeds

1 large green apple, cored

1 tbsp of fresh mint, chopped

2 oz of water

Preparation:

Peel the papaya and cut lengthwise in half. Scoop out the black seeds and flesh using a spoon. Cut into small chunks and set aside.

Cut the top of the pomegranate fruit using a sharp knife. Slice down to each of the white membranes inside of the fruit. Pop the seeds into a measuring cup and set aside.

Wash the apple and cut in half. Using a sharp knife, remove the core and cut into bite-sized pieces. Set aside.

Now, combine papaya, pomegranate, apple, and mint in a juicer. Process until well juiced and transfer to serving glasses. Stir in the water and refrigerate for 15 minutes before serving.

Nutritional information per serving: Kcal: 438, Protein: 6.1g, Carbs: 129g, Fats: 3.4g

11. Plum Blackberry Juice

Ingredients:

5 large plums, pitted

2 cups of blackberries

1 large lemon, peeled

1 cup of black grapes

1 medium-sized Golden delicious apple, cored

2 oz of water

1 tsp of liquid honey

Preparation:

Wash the plums and cut in half. Remove the pits and cut in small pieces. Set aside.

Wash the blackberries thoroughly under cold running water. Drain and set aside.

Peel the lemon and cut lengthwise in half. Set aside.

Wash the black grapes and set aside.

Wash the apple and cut in half. Remove the core and cut into bite-sized pieces. Set aside.

Now, combine plums, blackberries, lemon, black grapes, and apple in a juicer. Process until well juiced and transfer to serving glasses. Stir in the honey and water. Add some ice and serve immediately.

Enjoy!

Nutritional information per serving: Kcal: 344, Protein: 8g, Carbs: 110g, Fats: 3.1g

12. Pineapple Lime Juice

Ingredients:

1 cup of pineapple chunks

2 large limes, peeled

1 cup of guava, chopped

1 large cucumber, sliced

1 tbsp of fresh basil, chopped

2 oz of water

Preparation:

Cut the top of a pineapple and peel it using a sharp knife. Cut into small chunks and fill the measuring cup. Reserve the rest of the pineapple in a refrigerator.

Peel the limes and cut lengthwise in half. Set aside.

Wash the guava and cut into chunks. Fill the measuring cup and reserve the rest for some other recipe in a refrigerator.

Wash the cucumber and cut into thin slices. Set aside.

Now, combine pineapple, limes, guava, cucumber, and basil in a juicer. Process until well juiced and transfer to serving glasses. Stir in the water and refrigerate for 15

minutes before serving.

Nutritional information per serving: Kcal: 158, Protein: 4.7g, Carbs: 47.9g, Fats: 1.1g

13. Cranberry Pear Juice

Ingredients:

1 cup of cranberries

1 large pear, cored

1 large green apple, cored

3 large strawberries, chopped

1 large orange, peeled

¼ tsp of nutmeg, ground

2 oz of coconut water

Preparation:

Wash the cranberries thoroughly under cold running water. Drain and set aside.

Wash the pear and cut lengthwise in half. Remove the core and cut into bite-sized pieces. Set aside.

Wash the apple and cut in half. Remove the core and cut into bite-sized pieces. Set aside.

Wash the strawberries thoroughly and chop into small pieces. Set aside.

Peel the orange and divide into wedges. Set aside.

Now, combine pear, apple, strawberries, orange, and nutmeg in a juicer. Process until well juiced and transfer to serving glasses. Stir in the water and refrigerate or add some ice before serving.

Nutritional information per serving: Kcal: 158, Protein: 4.7g, Carbs: 47.9g, Fats: 1.1g

14. Carrot Orange Juice

Ingredients:

5 large carrots, peeled

1 large orange, peeled and wedged

1 large lemon, peeled

1 cup of Romaine lettuce, torn

1 large cucumber, sliced

¼ tsp of turmeric, ground

Preparation:

Peel and wash the carrots. Cut into thin slices and set aside.

Peel the orange and divide into wedges. Set aside.

Peel the lemon and cut lengthwise in half. Set aside.

Wash the lettuce thoroughly and torn with hands. Set aside.

Wash the cucumber and cut into thin slices. Set aside.

Now, combine carrots, orange, lemon, lettuce, and cucumber in a juicer. Process until well juiced and transfer to serving glasses. Stir in the turmeric and add some ice before serving. Enjoy!

Nutritional information per serving: Kcal: 232, Protein: 8.2g, Carbs: 74g, Fats: 1.7g

15. Asparagus Collard Greens Juice

Ingredients:

1 cup of asparagus, trimmed

1 cup of collard greens, torn

1 cup of watercress, torn

1 green bell pepper, chopped

1 large cucumber, sliced

2 oz of water

¼ tsp of salt

Preparation:

Wash the asparagus and trim off the woody ends. Cut into bite-sized pieces and fill the measuring cup. Reserve the rest for some other juice.

Combine collard greens and watercress in a colander. Wash thoroughly under cold running water and torn with hands. Set aside.

Wash the bell pepper and lengthwise in half. Remove the seeds and chop into small pieces. Set aside.

Wash the cucumber and cut into thin slices. Set aside.

Now, combine asparagus, collard greens, bell pepper, and cucumber in a juicer and process until well juiced. Transfer to serving glasses and stir in the salt and water. Refrigerate for 15 minutes before serving.

Nutritional information per serving: Kcal: 86, Protein: 8.2g, Carbs: 26.1g, Fats: 1g

16. Sweet Potato Green Smoothie

Ingredients:

1 cup of sweet potatoes, peeled

1 large fennel, chopped

1 cup of Swiss chard, torn

1 cup of red leaf lettuce, torn

1 cup of fresh spinach, torn

1 small cauliflower head, chopped

1 large lemon, peeled

Preparation:

Peel the sweet potato and cut into small chunks. Fill the measuring cup and reserve the rest for some other juice.

Wash the fennel bulb and trim off the wilted outer layers. Cut into small chunks and set aside.

Combine Swiss chard, red leaf lettuce, and spinach in a colander. Wash under cold running water and drain. Torn with hands and set aside.

Trim off the outer leaves of cauliflower. Wash it and cut into small pieces. Set aside.

Peel the lemon and cut lengthwise in half. Set aside.

Now, combine potato, fennel, Swiss chard, cauliflower, and lemon in a juicer and process until well juiced. Transfer to serving glasses and add some ice before serving.

Nutritional information per serving: Kcal: 218, Protein: 14.3g, Carbs: 67.7g, Fats: 1.9g

17. Fennel Brussels Sprouts Juice

Ingredients:

1 medium-sized fennel bulb, chopped

1 cup of Brussels sprouts, halved

1 large yellow bell pepper, chopped

1 large cucumber, sliced

¼ tsp of salt

2 oz of water

Preparation:

Trimm off the fennel stalks and wilted outer layers. Cut into bite-sized pieces and set aside.

Trim off the outer leaves and wash the Brussels sprouts. Cut in half and set aside.

Wash the bell pepper and cut lengthwise in half. Remove the seeds and chop into small pieces. Set aside.

Wash the cucumber and cut into thin slices. Set aside.

Now, combine fennel, Brussels sprouts, bell peppers, and cucumber in a juicer. Process until well juiced and stir in the salt and water. Refrigerate for 10 minutes before serving.

Nutritional information per serving: Kcal: 151, Protein: 9.7g, Carbs: 47.6g, Fats: 1.4g

18. Watermelon Peach Juice

Ingredients:

1 cup of watermelon, cubed

2 large peaches, pitted

1 large green apple, cored

5 fresh cherries, pitted

3 oz of coconut water

Preparation:

Cut the watermelon lengthwise. For one cup, you will need about one large wedge. Peel and cut into chunks. Remove the seeds and set aside. Reserve the rest of the melon for some other juices.

Wash the peaches and cut in half. Remove the pits and cut into bite-sized pieces. Set aside.

Wash the apple and cut in half. Remove the core and cut into bite-sized pieces. Set aside.

Wash the cherries and cut in half. Remove the pits and set aside.

Now, process watermelon, peaches, apple, and cherries in

a juicer. Transfer to serving glasses and stir in the coconut water. Add some ice and serve immediately.

Nutritional information per serving: Kcal: 276, Protein: 5.4g, Carbs: 47.6g, Fats: 1.6g

19. Spinach Apple Juice

Ingredients:

1 cup of fresh spinach, torn

1 large red apple, cored

1 cup of wild asparagus, trimmed

1 cup of collard greens, torn

1 cup of mustard greens, torn

2 oz of water

Preparation:

Combine spinach, collard greens, and mustard greens in a large colander. Wash under cold running water and drain. Torn with hands and set aside.

Wash the apple and cut in half. Remove the core and cut into bite-sized pieces. Set aside.

Now, combine spinach, collard greens, mustard greens, and apple in a juicer and process until well juiced. Transfer to serving glasses and stir in the water. Refrigerate for 15 minutes before serving.

Enjoy!

Nutritional information per serving: Kcal: 207, Protein: 16.1g, Carbs: 58.6g, Fats: 2.5g

20. Plum Cabbage Juice

Ingredients:

5 large plums, pitted

1 cup of purple cabbage, chopped

1 cup of blackberries

1 large cucumber, sliced

2 oz of water

Preparation:

Wash the plums and cut in half. Remove the pits and cut into quarters. Set aside.

Wash the cabbage thoroughly under cold running water. Drain and roughly chop it. Set aside.

Wash the blackberries under cold running water using a colander. Slightly drain and set aside.

Wash the cucumber and cut into thin slices. Set aside.

Now, combine plums, cabbage, blackberries, and cucumber in a juicer and process until juice. Transfer to serving glasses and stir in the water. Refrigerate for 15 minutes before serving.

Nutritional information per serving: Kcal: 221, Protein: 7.5g, Carbs: 69.1g, Fats: 2.1g

21. Crookneck Squash Tomato Juice

Ingredients:

1 cup of crookneck squash, chopped

1 large tomato, chopped

1 large lemon, peeled

1 large orange, peeled

1 large pear, cored and chopped

2 oz of water

1 tsp of liquid honey

Preparation:

Wash the crookneck squash and cut in half. Scoop out the seeds using a spoon. Cut into small chunks and fill the measuring cup. Reserve the rest for another juice.

Wash the tomato and place it in a bowl. Cut into bite-sized pieces and reserve the juice while cutting. Set aside.

Peel the lemon and cut lengthwise in half. Set aside.

Peel the orange and divide into wedges. Set aside.

Wash the pear and cut lengthwise in half. Remove the core

and cut into bite-sized pieces. Set aside.

Now, combine crookneck squash, tomato, lemon, orange, and pear in a juicer. Process until well juiced and transfer to serving glasses. Stir in the water and honey. Add some ice and serve immediately.

Nutritional information per serving: Kcal: 201, Protein: 5.9g, Carbs: 66.1g, Fats: 1.3g

22. Cauliflower Leek Juice

Ingredients:

1 small cauliflower head, chopped

3 large leeks, chopped

1 large lime, peeled

1 large zucchini, chopped

2 oz of water

Preparation:

Trim off the outer leaves of cauliflower. Wash it and cut into small pieces. Set aside.

Wash the leeks and cut into small pieces. Set aside.

Peel the lime and cut lengthwise in half. Set aside.

Peel the zucchini and cut in half. Scrape out the seeds and cut into small chunks. Set aside.

Now, combine cauliflower, leeks, lime, and zucchini in a juicer. Process until well juiced and stir in the water. Refrigerate for 10 minutes before serving.

Enjoy!

Nutritional information per serving: Kcal: 241, Protein: 13.2g, Carbs: 64.7g, Fats: 2.6g

23. Raspberry Beet Juice

Ingredients:

2 cups of raspberries

1 large green apple, cored

1 cup of beets, chopped

1 cup of fresh basil, torn

1 large lemon, peeled

3 oz of water

Preparation:

Wash the raspberries under cold running water using a colander. Drain and set aside.

Wash the apple and cut in half. Remove the core and cut into bite-sized pieces. Set aside.

Wash the beets and trim off the green ends. Cut into small pieces and fill the measuring cup. Reserve the greens for some other juice.

Wash the basil thoroughly under cold running water and torn with hands. Set aside.

Peel the lemon and cut lengthwise in half. Set aside.

Now, combine raspberries, apple, beets, basil, and lemon in a juicer. Process until well juiced. Stir in the water and refrigerate for 10 minutes before serving.

Enjoy!

Nutritional information per serving: Kcal: 218, Protein: 7.5g, Carbs: 76.4g, Fats: 2.5g

24. Apricot Pomegranate Juice

Ingredients:

1 large apricot, pitted

1 cup of pomegranate seeds

1 large lemon, peeled

1 large orange, wedged

1 large carrot, peeled

2 oz of coconut water

Preparation:

Wash the apricot and cut in half. Remove the pit and cut into small pieces. Set aside.

Cut the top of the pomegranate fruit using a sharp knife. Slice down to each of the white membranes inside of the fruit. Pop the seeds into measuring cup and set aside.

Peel the lemon and cut lengthwise in half. Set aside.

Peel the orange and divide into wedges. Set aside.

Peel and wash the carrot. Cut into thin slices and set aside.

Now, combine apricot, pomegranate seeds, lemon, orange,

and carrot in a juicer. Process until well juiced and transfer to serving glasses. Stir in the coconut water and add few ice cubes before serving.

Nutritional information per serving: Kcal: 241, Protein: 7.3g, Carbs: 73.9g, Fats: 2.3g

25. Broccoli Kale Juice

Ingredients:

2 cups of broccoli, trimmed

1 cup of fresh kale, torn

1 cup of fresh parsley, torn

1 large green apple, chopped

1 cup of fresh spinach, torn

2 oz of water

Preparation:

Wash the broccoli under cold running water and cut into small pieces. Set aside.

Combine parsley, kale, and spinach in a colander and wash under cold running water. Drain and torn with hands. Set aside.

Wash the apple and cut in half. Remove the core and cut into bite-sized pieces. Set aside.

Now, combine broccoli, kale, parsley, apple, and spinach in a juicer. Process until well juiced and stir in the water.

Refrigerate for 20 minutes before serving.

Nutritional information per serving: Kcal: 223, Protein: 20.4g, Carbs: 62.1g, Fats: 3.5g

26. Mango Cherry Juice

Ingredients:

1 cup of mango, chopped

1 cup of fresh cherries, pitted

2 cup of green grapes

1 large lemon, peeled

2 oz of water

Preparation:

Wash the mango and cut into chunks. Fill the measuring cup and reserve the rest for some other juice. Set aside.

Wash the cherries and cut in half. Remove the pits and set aside.

Wash the grapes and fill the measuring cup. Reserve the rest for some other juice. Set aside.

Peel the lemon and cut lengthwise in half. Set aside.

Now, combine mango, cherries, grapes, and lemon in a juicer and process until well juiced. Transfer to serving glasses and stir in the water.

Add few ice cubes and serve immediately.

Nutritional information per serving: Kcal: 302, Protein: 4.8g, Carbs: 86.3g, Fats: 1.7g

27. Grapefruit Apple Juice

Ingredients:

2 large grapefruits, peeled

1 large red apple, cored

2 large strawberries, chopped

1 small ginger knob, peeled

2 oz of coconut water

Preparation:

Peel the grapefruits and divide into wedges. Set aside.

Wash the apple and cut in half. Remove the core and cut into bite-sized pieces. Set aside.

Wash the strawberries and cut into small pieces. Set aside.

Peel the ginger knob and set aside.

Now, combine grapefruits, apple, strawberries, and ginger in a juicer. Process until well juiced and transfer to serving glasses. Stir in the coconut water and refrigerate for 15 minutes, or add some ice before serving.

Nutritional information per serving: Kcal: 302, Protein: 4.8g, Carbs: 86.3g, Fats: 1.7g

28. Pumpkin Nutmeg Juice

Ingredients:

2 cups of pumpkin, cubed

1 large green apple, cored

1 large cucumber, sliced

1 cup of Swiss chard, torn

2 oz of water

¼ tsp of nutmeg, ground

Preparation:

Peel the pumpkin and cut in half. Scoop out the seeds using a spoon. Cut one large wedge and peel it. Cut into small cubes and fill the measuring cup. Reserve the rest for some other juice.

Wash the apple and cut in half. Remove the core and cut into bite-sized pieces. Set aside.

Wash the cucumber and cut into thin slices. Set aside.

Wash the Swiss chard thoroughly under cold running water. Drain and torn with hands. Set aside.

Now, combine pumpkin, apple, cucumber, and Swiss

chards in a juicer. Process until well juiced and stir in the water and nutmeg. Refrigerate for 15 minutes before serving.

Nutritional information per serving: Kcal: 196, Protein: 5.8g, Carbs: 55.4g, Fats: 1.1g

29. Celery Green Bean Juice

Ingredients:

2 cups of celery, chopped

1 cup of green beans, chopped

1 cup of fresh mint, torn

1 cup of beet greens, torn

1 large cucumber, sliced

2 oz of water

¼ tsp of salt

Preparation:

Wash the celery and cut into small pieces. Set aside.

Wash the green beans and cut into bite-sized pieces. Set aside.

Combine mint and beet greens in a colander. Wash under cold running water and torn with hands. Set aside.

Wash the cucumber and cut into thin slices. Set aside.

Now, combine celery, green beans, mint, beet greens, and cucumber in a juicer. Process until well juiced and transfer to serving glasses. Stir in the water and salt.

Refrigerate for 10 minutes before serving.

Nutritional information per serving: Kcal: 91, Protein: 6.1g, Carbs: 26.1g, Fats: 1g

30. Strawberry Peach Juice

Ingredients:

1 cup of strawberries, chopped

2 large peaches, pitted

1 large green apple, cored

1 large lemon, peeled

1 large kiwi, peeled

1 large orange, peeled

2 oz of water

Preparation:

Wash the strawberries under cold running water. Remove the green parts and cut into bite-sized pieces. Set aside.

Wash the peaches and cut in half. Remove the pits and cut into small pieces. Set aside.

Wash the apple and cut half. Remove the core and cut into bite-sized pieces. Set aside.

Peel the lemon and kiwi. Cut lengthwise in half and set aside.

Now, combine strawberries, peaches, apple, lemon, and kiwi in a juicer and process until well juiced. Transfer to serving glasses and stir in the water. Add some ice and serve immediately.

Enjoy!

Nutritional information per serving: Kcal: 345, Protein: 7.8g, Carbs: 105g, Fats: 2.3g

31. Sour Pepper Lemon Juice

Ingredients:

1 large red bell pepper, chopped

1 large lemon, peeled

1 cup of beets, chopped

1 large cucumber, sliced

1 tsp of balsamic vinegar

¼ tsp of salt

2 oz of water

Preparation:

Wash the bell pepper and cut in half. Remove the seeds and chop into small pieces. Set aside.

Peel the lemon and cut lengthwise in half. Set aside.

Wash the beets and trim off the green ends. Cut into bite-sized pieces and fill the measuring cup. Reserve the rest for some other juice. Set aside.

Wash the cucumber and cut into thin slices. Set aside.

Now, combine bell pepper, lemon, beets, and cucumber in

a juicer. Process until well juiced and transfer to serving glasses. Stir in the balsamic vinegar, salt, and water.

Refrigerate for 20 minutes before serving.

Nutritional information per serving: Kcal: 130, Protein: 6.4g, Carbs: 39.2g, Fats: 1.2g

32. Blackberry Apricot Juice

Ingredients:

1 cup of blackberries

1 cup of raspberries

3 large apricots, pitted

1 large red apple, cored

3 large carrots, peeled

Preparation:

Combine blackberries and raspberries in a colander. Wash under cold running water and slightly drain. Set aside.

Wash the apricots and cut in half. Remove the pits and cut into bite-sized pieces. Set aside.

Wash the apple and cut in half. Remove the core and cut into small pieces.

Wash and peel the carrots. Cut into thin slices and set aside.

Now, combine blackberries, raspberries, apricots, apple, and carrots in a juicer. Process until well juiced and transfer to serving glasses. Stir in the water and refrigerate for 20

minutes before serving.

Enjoy!

Nutritional information per serving: Kcal: 301, Protein: 7.6g, Carbs: 97.4g, Fats: 2.9g

33. Strawberry Avocado Juice

Ingredients:

5 large strawberries, chopped

1 cup of avocado, pitted

1 cup of fresh mint, chopped

1 large apple, cored

1 large lemon, peeled

1 large cucumber, sliced

Preparation:

Wash the strawberries and cut into small pieces. Set aside.

Peel the avocado and cut lengthwise in half. Remove the pit and cut into chunks and fill the measuring cup. Reserve the rest for later.

Wash the mint thoroughly and torn with hands. Set aside.

Wash the apple and cut in half. Remove the core and cut into bite-sized pieces. Set aside.

Peel the lemon and cut lengthwise in half. Set aside.

Wash the cucumber and cut into thin slices. Set aside.

Now, combine strawberries, avocado, mint, lemon, and cucumber in a juicer and process until juiced. Transfer to serving glasses and stir in the water. Add some ice and serve immediately.

Nutritional information per serving: Kcal: 376, Protein: 8.1g, Carbs: 67.8g, Fats: 23.3g

34. Cantaloupe Carrot Juice

Ingredients:

1 cup of cantaloupe, cubed

3 large carrots, sliced

1 large orange, peeled

1 large green apple, cored

2 oz of coconut water

Preparation:

Cut the cantaloupe in half. Scoop out the seeds and flesh. Cut two wedges and peel them. Chop into cubes and set aside. Reserve the rest of the cantaloupe in a refrigerator.

Wash and peel the carrots. Cut into thin slices and set aside.

Peel the orange and divide into wedges. Set aside.

Wash the apple and cut in half. Remove the core and cut into bite-sized pieces. Set aside.

Now, combine cantaloupe, carrots, orange, and apple in a juicer. Process until well juiced and stir in the coconut water.

Nutritional information per serving: Kcal: 277, Protein: 6g, Carbs: 83g, Fats: 1.4g

35. Pomegranate Pepper Juice

Ingredients:

1 cup of pomegranate seeds

1 large red bell pepper, chopped

1 cup of cranberries

4 large plums, pitted

1 large green apple, cored

Preparation:

Cut the top of the pomegranate fruit using a sharp knife. Slice down to each of the white membranes inside of the fruit. Pop the seeds into a measuring cup and set aside.

Wash the bell pepper and cut lengthwise in half. Remove the seeds and cut into small pieces. Set aside.

Wash the cranberries thoroughly and drain. Set aside.

Wash the plums and cut in half. Remove the pits and cut into bite-sized pieces. Set aside.

Wash the apple and cut in half. Remove the core and cut into bite-sized pieces. Set aside.

Now, combine pomegranate, cranberries, plums, and

apple in a juicer. Process until well juiced and add some ice before serving.

Enjoy!

Nutritional information per serving: Kcal: 277, Protein: 6g, Carbs: 83g, Fats: 1.4g

36. Zucchini Kiwi Juice

Ingredients:

1 large zucchini, seeded

3 large kiwis, peeled

1 large lime, peeled

1 cup of pomegranate seeds

1 large orange, peeled

Preparation:

Wash the zucchini and cut in half. Scoop out the seeds using a spoon. Cut into small chunks and set aside.

Peel the kiwis and lime. Cut lengthwise in half and set aside.

Cut the top of the pomegranate fruit using a sharp knife. Slice down to each of the white membranes inside of the fruit. Pop the seeds into a measuring cup and set aside.

Peel the orange and divide into wedges. Set aside.

Now, process kiwis, zucchini, lime, pomegranate seeds, and orange in a juicer.

Transfer to a serving glasses and add some ice cubes before serving.

Nutritional information per serving: Kcal: 183, Protein: 8.5g, Carbs: 52.6g, Fats: 1.6g

37. Blueberry Mango Juice

Ingredients:

1 cup of mango, chopped

1 cup of blueberries

1 large cucumber, sliced

1 large green apple, cored

2 oz of water

Preparation:

Wash the mango and cut into chunks. Fill the measuring cup and reserve the rest for some other juice. Set aside.

Place the blueberries in a colander and wash under cold running water. Drain and set aside.

Wash the apple and remove the core. Cut into bite-sized pieces and set aside.

Now, combine mango, blueberries, and apple in a juicer and process until juiced.

Transfer to serving glasses and stir in the water. Add some ice before serving and enjoy!

Nutritional information per serving: Kcal: 180, Protein: 5.9g, Carbs: 63.5g, Fats: 1.1g

38. Carrot Lemon Juice

Ingredients:

5 large carrots, sliced

2 large lemons, peeled

1 large green apple, cored

1 cup of Romaine lettuce

2 oz of water

Preparation:

Wash the carrots and cut into thick slices. Set aside.

Peel the lemons and cut lengthwise in half. Set aside.

Wash the apple and remove the core. Cut into bite-sized pieces and set aside.

Wash the lettuce thoroughly under cold running water. Torn with hands and set aside.

Now, process carrots, lettuce, lemon, and apple in a juicer. Transfer to serving glasses and add some ice before serving.

Enjoy!

Nutritional information per serving: Kcal: 232, Protein: 6.1g, Carbs: 74.9g, Fats: 1.7g

39. Guava Lime Juice

Ingredients:

1 large guava, peeled

1 large lime, peeled

2 large oranges, peeled

1 large cucumber, sliced

2 oz of water

Preparation:

Peel and wash the guava. Cut into small chunks and set aside.

Peel the lime and cut lengthwise in half. Set aside.

Peel the oranges and divide into wedges. Set aside.

Wash the cucumber and cut into thin slices. Set aside.

Now, combine lime, guava, orange, and cucumber in a juicer and process until juiced.

Transfer to serving glasses and stir in the water. Add some ice and serve immediately.

Nutritional information per serving: Kcal: 210, Protein: 7g, Carbs: 65.7g, Fats: 1.3g

40. Celery Lemon Juice

Ingredients:

1 large lemon, peeled

1 cup of celery, chopped

1 cup of fresh mint, chopped

1 cup of fresh spinach, chopped

2 oz of water

Preparation:

Peel the lemon and cut lengthwise in half. Set aside.

Wash the celery stalks and chop into small pieces. Fill the measuring cup and set aside.

Wash the spinach and mint in a colander. Chop and place in a medium bowl. Set aside.

Now, combine lemon, celery, mint, and spinach in a juicer and process until juiced. Transfer to serving glasses and stir in the water.

Refrigerate for 10 minutes before serving.

Nutritional information per serving: Kcal: 35, Protein: 3.1g, Carbs: 13.2g, Fats: 0.7g

41. Basil Lemon Juice

Ingredients:

1 cup of fresh basil, chopped

1 large lemon, peeled

1 cup of Swiss chard, chopped

1 large green apple, cored

1 cup of fresh mint, chopped

2 oz of water

Preparation:

Combine basil, Swiss chard, and mint in a large colander. Wash thoroughly under cold running water. Chop into small pieces and set aside. Peel the lemon and cut lengthwise in half. Wash the apple and cut in half. Remove the core and cut into bite-sized pieces. Set aside.

Now, combine basil, Swiss chard, mint, lemon, and apple in a juicer and process until well juiced. Transfer to serving glasses and stir in the water. Refrigerate for 10 minutes before serving. Enjoy!

Nutritional information per serving: Kcal: 126, Protein: 3.9g, Carbs: 39.1g, Fats: 1.1g

42. Pineapple Carrot Juice

Ingredients:

1 cup of pineapple chunks

2 large carrots, sliced

1 cup of watercress, torn

1 large lime, peeled

1 small ginger knob, peeled

2 oz of water

Preparation:

Peel the pineapple and cut into small chunks. Set aside.

Wash and peel the carrots. Cut into thin slices and set aside.

Wash the watercress thoroughly under cold running water. Torn with hands and set aside.

Peel the lime and cut lengthwise in half. Set aside.

Peel the ginger root knob and cut into small pieces. Set aside.

Now, combine pineapple, carrots, watercress, lemon, and

ginger in a juicer and process until well juiced.

Transfer to serving glasses and stir in water.

Add some ice and serve.

Nutritional information per serving: Kcal: 135, Protein: 3.3g, Carbs: 40.6g, Fats: 3.3g

43. Orange Apple Juice

Ingredients:

3 large oranges, peeled

1 large green apple, cored

1 cup of fresh asparagus, trimmed

¼ tsp of turmeric, ground

2 oz of water

Preparation:

Peel the oranges and divide into wedges. Set aside.

Wash the apple and remove the core. Cut into bite-sized pieces and set aside.

Wash the asparagus thoroughly under cold running water and trim off the woody ends. Cut into small pieces and set aside.

Now, combine oranges, apple, and asparagus in a juicer and process until juiced. Transfer to serving glasses and stir in the turmeric and water.

Refrigerate for 10 minutes before serving.

Nutritional information per serving: Kcal: 316, Protein: 9.1g, Carbs: 98.1g, Fats: 1.2g

44. Grapefruit Kiwi Juice

Ingredients:

2 large grapefruits, peeled

1 large kiwi, peeled

1 large lime, peeled

2 large celery stalks, chopped

1 cup of red leaf lettuce, chopped

2 oz of water

Preparation:

Peel the grapefruit and divide into wedges. Set aside.

Peel the kiwi and lime. Cut in half and set aside.

Wash and chop the celery stalks into small pieces. Set aside.

Wash the lettuce thoroughly under cold running water and roughly chop it. Set aside.

Now, combine grapefruit, kiwi, celery, and lettuce in a juicer and process until well juiced.

Transfer to serving glasses and stir in the water. Serve

immediately.

Nutritional information per serving: Kcal: 233, Protein: 6g, Carbs: 70.7g, Fats: 1.3g

SALAD RECIPES

1. **Smoked Salmon Salad**

Ingredients:

4 oz. smoked salmon, sliced

½ red onion, sliced

1 cup Iceberg lettuce, roughly chopped

¼ cup Feta cheese, crumbled

¼ cup Kalamata olives, pitted

1 tbsp. extra-virgin olive oil

¼ tsp. garlic powder

½ tsp. dried thyme

¼ tsp. dried rosemary

¼ tsp. sea salt

¼ tsp. black pepper, ground

Preparation:

In a small bowl, combine olive oil, garlic powder, thyme,

rosemary, salt, and pepper. Stir until well combined and set aside.

Rinse and drain the lettuce. Roughly chop and place in a large bowl. Top with onions, salmon, and cheese.

Drizzle with previously prepared dressing and serve immediately.

Optionally, sprinkle with some fresh lemon juice for some extra taste.

Enjoy!

Nutritional information per serving: Kcal: 213, Protein: 13.7g, Carbs: 5.9g, Fats: 15.4g

2. Spinach Mushroom Salad

Ingredients:

4 cups fresh spinach, rinsed

2 cups button mushrooms

1 medium-sized red onion, thinly sliced

3 tbsp. olive oil

1 tsp. coconut sugar

¼ cup balsamic vinegar

½ tsp. salt

¼ tsp. black pepper, ground

Preparation:

In a small skillet, combine balsamic vinegar, coconut sugar, salt, and pepper. Bring it to a boil and remove from the heat immediately. Let it chill completely and then add sliced onions. Cover with a lid and refrigerate for later.

Now, preheat the oil in a large skillet over medium-high heat. Add mushrooms and sprinkle with some salt and pepper to taste. Cook for 10 minutes, stirring occasionally.

Add one cup of spinach to the skillet and cook for 1-2

minutes, or until the spinach has been wilted. Remove from the heat and set aside.

Arrange the remaining spinach on a serving plate and top with mushroom and spinach mixture. Add onions and remaining marinade.

Serve immediately.

Nutritional information per serving: Kcal: 243, Protein: 4.6g, Carbs: 11.5g, Fats: 21.5g

3.   Green Bean Salad with Baby Potatoes

Ingredients:

2 cups fresh green beans

1 cup baby potatoes, peeled

1 small red onion, sliced

3 tbsp. olive oil

2 tsp. yellow mustard

1 tsp. fresh thyme, finely chopped

2 tsp. lemon juice, freshly squeezed

¼ tsp. salt

¼ tsp. black pepper

Preparation:

In a small mixing bowl, combine olive oil, yellow mustard, thyme, lemon juice, salt, and pepper. Mix until well combined and set aside.

Place the green beans in a deep pot and add water enough to cover. Sprinkle with some salt and bring it to a simmer. Cook for 2-3 minutes, or until almost tender. Remove from the heat. Using a large mesh skimmer, transfer to a large bowl and set aside.

Place the potatoes to the same pot and bring it to a boil over medium-high heat. Simmer for 10-12 minutes, or until fork-tender. Remove from the heat and drain. Cut into bite-sized pieces and add to the bowl with green beans.

Add onions and drizzle all with previously prepared dressing. Gently toss until well incorporated and serve immediately.

Nutritional information per serving: Kcal: 246, Protein: 3.2g, Carbs: 14.3g, Fats: 21.5g

4. Frisee Arugula Salad

Ingredients:

3 cups fresh frisee, torn

2 cups arugula, torn

1 tbsp. lemon juice, freshly squeezed

1 tsp. Dijon mustard

1 tbsp. olive oil

½ tsp. salt

¼ tsp. black pepper, ground

½ tsp. Italian seasoning

Preparation:

Combine all greens in a large colander. Rinse under cold running water and drain. Chop into bite-sized pieces and transfer to a large bowl. Set aside.

In a small bowl, combine lemon juice, Dijon mustard, olive oil, salt, pepper and Italian seasoning. Mix until well combined and drizzle over the salad.

You can add some more greens of your choice, such as spinach, kale, or watercress. However, it's optional.

Serve immediately.

Nutritional information per serving: Kcal: 246, Protein: 3.2g, Carbs: 14.3g, Fats: 21.5g

5. Sweet Buckwheat Salad with Avocado and Spinach

Ingredients:

1 cup buckwheat groats

½ ripe avocado, peeled and sliced

1 cup fresh spinach, rinsed and chopped

½ medium-sized cucumber, sliced

½ cup black beans, soaked overnight

1 whole lime, juiced

1 tbsp. olive oil

1 tsp. maple syrup

¼ tsp. cumin powder

¼ tsp. cayenne pepper

Salt and pepper to taste

Preparation:

Place the buckwheat in a heavy-bottomed pot and add 2 cups of water. Bring it to a boil over medium-high heat. Cook for 10-15 minutes, or until tender. Remove from the heat and drain the excess liquid. Set aside.

Drain the beans and place them in a pot. Add water enough to cover all and bring it to a boil. Cook for 30 minutes. Remove from the heat and drain. Set aside.

Using a large colander, rinse the spinach under cold running water. Drain and transfer to a large bowl. Add cooked buckwheat, cooked beans, avocado, and sliced cucumber.

In a small bowl, combine olive oil, lime juice, maple syrup, cumin powder, cayenne pepper, salt, and pepper. Stir well until combined and drizzle over the salad.

Serve immediately.

Nutritional information per serving: Kcal: 287, Protein: 10.2g, Carbs: 38.1g, Fats: 12.2g

6. Fried Red Bell Pepper Salad

Ingredients:

5 medium-sized red bell peppers, halved lengthwise and seeds removed

1 garlic clove, minced

1 tbsp. capers, drained

¼ cup olives, pitted

1 tbsp. balsamic vinegar

2 tbsp. extra-virgin olive oil

1 tbsp. fresh parsley, finely chopped

1 tsp. sea salt

Preparation:

In a small bowl, combine garlic, capers, olives, balsamic vinegar, parsley, salt, and one tablespoon of oil. Stir well and set aside for 15 minutes before use.

Grease a large non-stick pan with the remaining olive oil. Heat up over medium-high heat. Add bell peppers and sprinkle with some salt. Cook for 5 minutes, or until tender and brown on the edges. Remove from the heat and transfer to a large bowl.

Top with previously prepared mixture and sprinkle with finely chopped parsley before serving.

Nutritional information per serving: Kcal: 240, Protein: 3.4g, Carbs: 24.5g, Fats: 16.6g

7. Cheesy Chicken Salad

Ingredients:

1 lb. chicken breast, skinless and boneless

¼ cup cottage cheese, crumbled

1 medium-sized red bell pepper, chopped

1 small cucumber, sliced

1 small red onion, chopped

2 cups Romaine lettuce, chopped

1 tsp. lemon juice, freshly squeezed

1 tsp. Worcestershire sauce

1 tbsp. olive oil

½ tsp. dried thyme, ground

¼ tsp. smoked paprika

¼ tsp. garlic powder

Salt to taste

Preparation:

Rinse well the chicken and pat-dry with a kitchen paper.

Transfer to cutting board and cut into bite-sized pieces. Set aside.

Preheat the oil in a saucepan over medium-high heat. Add chicken and sprinkle with garlic powder, thyme, smoked paprika, and salt to taste. Cook for 5-7 minutes, or until golden brown. Remove from the heat and set aside.

Rinse the lettuce under cold running water. Chop into bite-sized pieces and place in large bowl along with cottage cheese, cucumber, bell pepper, and onion.

Sprinkle all with Worcestershire sauce and lemon juice. Give it a good stir and serve immediately.

Nutritional information per serving: Kcal: 275, Protein: 36.2g, Carbs: 11.4g, Fats: 9.2g

8. Sweet Potato Salad with Eggs

Ingredients:

2 medium-sized sweet potatoes

2 eggs

1 medium-sized onion, sliced

1 tbsp. olive oil

1 tbsp. fresh parsley, finely chopped

½ tsp. salt

½ tsp. black pepper, ground

¼ tsp. dried oregano, ground

¼ tsp. dried rosemary, ground

Preparation:

Place the eggs in a deep pot and add enough water to cover. Bring it to a boil and cook for 10 minutes. Remove from the heat and transfer immediately to ice cold water. Let it chill for a few minutes. Peel and cut into bite-sized pieces. Set aside.

Peel the potatoes and cut into bite-sized cubes.

Peel the onion and cut into thin slices. Set aside.

Place the sweet potatoes in a heavy-bottomed pot and cover with water. Bring it to a boil and cook for 7-10 minutes over a medium-high heat. Remove from the heat and drain well.

Preheat the oil in a large saucepan over medium-high heat. Add potatoes and sprinkle with salt, pepper, oregano, and rosemary. Cook for 2-3 minutes and remove from the heat.

Transfer the potatoes to a large bowl along with eggs, onion, and parsley. Stir until well incorporated.

Nutritional information per serving: Kcal: 217, Protein: 5.7g, Carbs: 32g, Fats: 7.9g

9. Greek Style Salad

Ingredients:

2 large tomatoes, chopped

¼ cup Feta cheese, crumbled

1 cucumber, sliced

1 medium-sized capsicum, chopped

1 small onion, chopped

¼ cup black olives, pitted

1 tbsp. olive oil

½ tsp. salt

½ tsp. black pepper, ground

Preparation:

Rinse the tomatoes and transfer to a cutting board. Cut into bite-sized pieces and set aside.

Wash the cucumber and cut into thin slices. Set aside.

Peel the onion and chop into small pieces. Place in a small bowl and add water enough to cover. Sprinkle with some salt and mix. Let it soak for 10 minutes. When done, drain and squeeze with your hands to remove the excess water.

Wash the pepper and cut lengthwise into halves. Remove the stem and seeds. Chop into small pieces and set aside.

Now, combine all prepared ingredients in a large bowl. Add olives and sprinkle all with olive oil, salt, and pepper to taste. Give it a good stir and serve immediately.

Nutritional information per serving: Kcal: 209, Protein: 6.3g, Carbs: 20g, Fats: 13.5g

10. Cabbage Radish Salad

Ingredients:

2 cups cabbage, shredded

2 medium-sized radishes, thinly sliced

1 medium-sized purple onion, sliced

2 eggs

1 tbsp. olive oil

1 tbsp. white wine vinegar

1 tsp. Italian seasoning

¼ tsp. black pepper, ground

Preparation:

Wash the radishes and trim off the green parts. Using a sharp knife, cut into thin slices and set aside.

Peel the onion and cut into thin slices. Sprinkle with some salt and set aside.

In a small mixing bowl, combine olive oil, vinegar, Italian seasoning, and pepper. Mix until well combined and set aside.

Place the eggs in a deep pot. Add water enough to cover and bring it to a boil over medium-high heat. Cook for 10 minutes and remove from the heat. Let it cool completely. Peel and cut into bite-sized pieces.

Now, combine cabbage, radishes, onion, and eggs in a large bowl. Drizzle with previously prepared dressing and serve immediately.

Nutritional information per serving: Kcal: 173, Protein: 7.1g, Carbs: 10.2g, Fats: 12.2g

11. Mediterranean Salad

Ingredients:

4 oz. shrimps, cleaned and deveined

1 cup cherry tomatoes, halved

1 medium-sized purple onion, sliced

1 green bell pepper, chopped

¼ cup green olives, pitted

½ ripe avocado, sliced

¼ cup goat's cheese crumbled

2 tbsp. olive oil

1 tsp. balsamic vinegar

½ tsp. sea salt

¼ tsp. dried thyme, ground

¼ tsp. dried oregano, ground

¼ tsp. black pepper

Preparation:

Preheat one tablespoon of olive oil in a large non-stick

skillet over medium-high heat. Add shrimps and sprinkle with some salt and pepper. Cook for 2-3 minutes on each side. Remove from the heat and set aside.

In a small mixing bowl, combine the remaining olive oil, balsamic vinegar, thyme, and oregano. Mix until combined and set aside.

Wash and prepare the vegetables.

Now, combine shrimps, cherry tomatoes, purple onion, green bell pepper, and olives in a large salad bowl. Drizzle all with previously prepared dressing and gently toss.

Finally top with cheese and avocado slices and serve immediately.

Enjoy!

Nutritional information per serving: Kcal: 304, Protein: 14.8g, Carbs: 13.9g, Fats: 22.4g

12. Rice Vegetable Salad

Ingredients:

½ cup brown rice, long-grain

2 tbsp. olive oil

½ cup cherry tomatoes, halved

1 small cucumber, cut into bite-sized cubes

2 oz. Feta cheese, crumbled

½ tbsp. sherry vinegar

1 small onion, finely chopped

1 garlic clove, minced

½ cup fresh mint, roughly chopped

½ cup fresh parsley, roughly chopped

Salt and pepper to taste

Preparation:

Preheat one tablespoon of olive oil in a saucepan over medium-high heat. Add minced garlic and finely chopped onions. Sprinkle with some salt and stir-fry for 3-4 minutes, or until translucent. Remove the mixture from the pan and set aside.

Add the remaining oil to the pan and heat up over medium-high heat. Add rice and fry for 2 minutes, or until slightly golden brown. Pour in 1 ½ cup of water and stir well. Bring it to a simmer and reduce the heat to low. Cook for 25-30 minutes, stirring occasionally. Remove from the heat and cover with a lid. Let it sit for 5 minutes.

Now, combine rice and onion mixture in a large bowl. Add tomatoes and cucumber. Sprinkle all with sherry vinegar, salt, and pepper to taste. Optionally, add some olive oil for extra flavor.

Finally, stir in the cheese, mint and parsley.

Serve immediately.

Nutritional information per serving: Kcal: 287, Protein: 7.1g, Carbs: 34.5g, Fats: 14.6g

13. Creamy Beet Salad

Ingredients:

6 oz. beets

1 egg, hard-boiled

½ cup Greek yogurt

2 tbsp. sour cream

2 tsp. yellow mustard

1 tbsp. fresh parsley, finely chopped

1 garlic clove, minced

2 walnuts, minced

2 tsp. pumpkin seeds

1 cup fresh arugula, roughly chopped

1 tbsp. olive oil

Salt

Preparation:

Trim off the green ends of the beets. Wash thoroughly and cut into thin slices. Place in a deep pot and add water enough to cover. Bring it to a boil over medium-high heat and cook for 15-20 minutes. Remove from the heat drain well. Set aside.

Heat up a non-stick skillet over medium-high heat. Add pumpkin seeds and stir-fry for 3-5 minutes, or until lightly toasted.

In a mixing bowl, combine Greek yogurt, sour cream, yellow mustard, and olive oil. Stir until combined and set aside.

Place the egg in a deep pot and add water enough to cover. Bring it to a boil over medium-high heat. Cook for 10-12 minutes. Remove from the heat and let it cool completely. Peel and chop into bite-sized pieces.

Now, combine beets, eggs, garlic, arugula, and pumpkin seeds. Add salt to taste and stir until well combined.

Pour over the yogurt mixture and stir once again before serving.

Enjoy!

Nutritional information per serving: Kcal: 265, Protein: 12.9g, Carbs: 13.7g, Fats: 19.1g

14. Lentil Tomato Salad

Ingredients:

1 cup lentils, drained

1 large Roma tomato, chopped

1 small Jalapeno pepper, finely chopped

1 garlic clove, minced

1 medium-sized cucumber, chopped

1 medium-sized purple onion, chopped

1 large red bell pepper, chopped

1 tbsp. olive oil

¼ tsp. cumin, ground

1 tbsp. lemon juice, freshly squeezed

Preparation:

Rinse the tomato and remove the stem. Chop into bite-sized pieces and set aside.

Wash the bell pepper and cut lengthwise in half. Remove the stem and seeds. Cut into bite-sized pieces and set aside.

Cut the cucumber into bite-sized pieces and set aside.

Peel the onion and chop into small pieces. Set aside.

Preheat the oil in a large saucepan over medium-high heat. Add garlic and Jalapeno pepper. Stir-fry for 2-3 minutes, or until golden.

Add lentils and sprinkle with cumin powder. Stir well and remove from the heat. Let it chill for a while and then transfer to a large bowl.

Now, add all vegetables to the bowl and drizzle with lemon juice. Toss to combine and serve immediately.

Nutritional information per serving: Kcal: 326, Protein: 18.8g, Carbs: 52.3g, Fats: 5.9g

15.   Caesar Salad

Ingredients:

4 oz. chicken filets, skinless and boneless, cut into 1-inch thick strips

½ medium-sized tomato, chopped

1 egg, hard-boiled

¼ cup croutons

1 small cucumber, sliced

1 cup Iceberg lettuce

2 tbsp. Greek yogurt

1 tbsp. goat's cheese, crumbled

1 tbsp. olive oil

Salt and pepper to taste

Preparation:

Rinse the chicken under cold running water and pat-dry with a kitchen paper. Transfer to a cutting board and cut into bite-sized pieces. Set aside.

Preheat the oil in a medium saucepan over medium-high

heat. Add chicken and sprinkle with some salt and pepper to taste. Cook for 5 minutes, or until golden brown and crispy on the edges. Remove from the heat and set aside.

In a small mixing bowl, combine Greek yogurt, goat's cheese, olive oil, salt, and pepper. Mix until well combined and set aside.

Place the egg in a deep pot and add enough water to cover. Bring to a boil and cook for 12 minutes. Remove from the heat and rinse with ice cold water. Peel and chop into bite-sized pieces.

Now, combine chicken, tomato, croutons, cucumber, and lettuce in a large bowl. Drizzle with previously prepared dressing and stir well.

Serve immediately.

Nutritional information per serving: Kcal: 309, Protein: 15.7g, Carbs: 19g, Fats: 19.4g

16. Spicy Avocado Couscous Salad

Ingredients:

1 ripe avocado, cut into bite-sized pieces

½ cup couscous

1 tbsp. parsley, finely chopped

½ cup canned lentils, rinsed and drained

1 tbsp. canned corn, drained and rinsed

1 large red bell pepper, chopped

3 tbsp. olive oil

1 small chili pepper, seeded

1 garlic clove

½ tsp. salt

½ tsp. smoked paprika

Preparation:

Place the couscous in a deep bowl and pour in 1 cup of boiling water. Cover with a lid and let it stand for 10 minutes.

Meanwhile, combine olive oil, chili pepper, garlic, salt, and smoked paprika in a food processor. Blend until smooth and pureed. Optionally, add bell pepper instead chili if it is too spicy for your taste.

Fluff the couscous with a fork and add lentils along with avocado, corn, parsley, corn, and bell pepper.

Finally, drizzle with sauce and give it a good stir.

Serve immediately.

Nutritional information per serving: Kcal: 323, Protein: 9.3g, Carbs: 36.4g, Fats: 17g

17. Shiitake Spinach Salad

Ingredients:

1 cup Shiitake mushrooms, chopped

2 cups fresh baby spinach, roughly chopped

¼ cup Feta cheese, crumbled

1 garlic clove, minced

2 small beets, sliced

1 small onion, sliced

1 tsp. fresh thyme, ground

2 tbsp. olive oil

½ tbsp. balsamic vinegar

Salt and pepper to taste

Preparation:

Preheat the oil in a large saucepan over medium-high heat. Add garlic and onions. Stir-fry for 3-4 minutes, or until translucent.

Add mushrooms and sprinkle with some thyme, salt, and pepper to taste. Cook for 3-4 minutes, or until slightly soften.

Throw in the spinach and stir well. Cook for 2-3 minutes more and sprinkle with balsamic vinegar. Stir well and remove from the heat.

Transfer all to a large salad bowl and top with sliced beets, onions, and cheese.

Serve immediately.

Nutritional information per serving: Kcal: 278, Protein: 6.9g, Carbs: 26g, Fats: 18.5g

18. Potato Salad with Creamy Dressing

Ingredients:

2 medium-sized potatoes, cut into bite-sized pieces

1 large red bell pepper, chopped

1 small cucumber, sliced

¼ cup spring onions, chopped

1 tsp. yellow mustard

4 tbsp. Greek yogurt

1 tsp. white wine vinegar

¼ tsp. black pepper, ground

½ tsp. salt

Preparation:

Place the potatoes in a deep pot and add enough water to cover. Bring to a boil over medium-high heat. Cook for 10-15 minutes, or until fork-tender. Remove from the heat and drain. Set aside.

In a small mixing bowl, combine Greek yogurt, white wine vinegar, yellow mustard, black pepper, and salt. Mix until well combined and set aside.

Now, place the potatoes in a salad bowl and drizzle over with yogurt dressing. Sprinkle with green onions before serving.

Enjoy!

Nutritional information per serving: Kcal: 202, Protein: 6.5g, Carbs: 45.1g, Fats: 0.8g

19. Simple Tomato Mozzarella Salad

Ingredients:

2 large tomatoes, cut into bite-sized pieces

½ cup Mozzarella cheese, sliced

½ small purple onion, finely chopped

¼ cup olives, pitted

2 tbsp. fresh parsley, finely chopped

½ tsp. dried oregano, ground

1 tbsp. extra-virgin olive oil

¼ tsp. sea salt

¼ tsp. black pepper

Preparation:

Rinse the tomatoes and cut into bite-sized pieces. Transfer to a salad bowl and add mozzarella cheese.

In a small mixing bowl, combine olive oil, dried oregano, sea salt, and black pepper. Mix until combined.

Drizzle the prepared salad with the dressing.

Sprinkle with parsley and top with olives before serving.

Enjoy!

Nutritional information per serving: Kcal: 285, Protein: 8.2g, Carbs: 21.3g, Fats: 21g

20. Bean Salad With Feta and Chia Seeds

Ingredients:

½ cup canned beans, drained and rinsed

1 small red onion, chopped

1 garlic clove, finely chopped

1 large tomato, chopped

¼ cup Feta cheese, crumbled

4 tsp. chia seeds

1 tsp. shallots, finely chopped

1 tbsp. fresh parsley, finely chopped

1 tsp. apple cider vinegar

1 tsp. yellow mustard

2 tbsp. olive oil

¼ tsp. cumin, ground

¼ tsp. dried oregano, ground

½ tsp. salt

¼ tsp. black pepper, ground

Preparation:

In a small mixing bowl, combine olive oil, apple cider vinegar, garlic, cumin, oregano, salt and pepper. Mix until well combined and set aside.

Place the beans in a large colander. Rinse under cold running water. Drain and transfer to a serving bowl.

Add tomato and onion. Drizzle with previously prepared mixture and give it a good stir.

Sprinkle with chia seeds and serve immediately.

Enjoy!

Nutritional information per serving: Kcal: 218, Protein: 4.8g, Carbs: 11.1g, Fats: 18.6g

21. Pepper Salad with Lentils

Ingredients:

4 large red bell peppers

½ cup lentils, drained

1 tbsp. fresh parsley, finely chopped

1 tbsp. fresh basil, finely chopped

1 tsp. fresh mint, finely chopped

¼ cup Feta cheese, cut into small cubes

2 tsp. balsamic vinegar

2 tbsp. olive oil

¼ tsp. cumin, ground

2-3 walnuts, chopped

¼ tsp. cayenne pepper

Preparation:

Preheat one tablespoon of olive oil in a large skillet over medium-high heat. Add peppers and sprinkle with some salt to taste. Cook for 3-4 minutes on each side, or until tender.

Rinse the lentils using a colander. Drain well and set aside.

Now, combine the remaining oil, balsamic vinegar, cumin, cayenne pepper, parsley, basil, and mint in a mixing bowl. Stir until well combined.

Combine peppers, lentils, and Feta cheese on a serving dish. Drizzle all with previously prepared dressing.

Top with walnuts and serve immediately.

Enjoy!

Nutritional information per serving: Kcal: 218, Protein: 4.8g, Carbs: 11.1g, Fats: 18.6g

22. Carrot Mustard Salad

Ingredients:

4 large carrots

1 tsp. yellow mustard

1 tsp. lemon juice, freshly squeezed

1 tbsp. olive oil

2 tbsp. fresh parsley, finely chopped

¼ tsp. dried thyme, ground

Salt and pepper

Preparation:

Rinse the carrot and gently peel the outer skin. Cut into thin slices and transfer to a salad bowl. Set aside.

In a small mixing bowl, combine yellow mustard, lemon juice, olive oil, and thyme. Add salt and pepper according to your taste. Mix until combined and drizzle over the carrots.

Give it a good stir and let it stand for 30 minutes before serving.

Enjoy!

Nutritional information per serving: Kcal: 246, Protein: 2.9g, Carbs: 29.4g, Fats: 14.3g

23. Tuna Rice Salad

Ingredients:

½ brown rice

4 oz. minced tuna, drained

1 tbsp. orange juice, freshly squeezed

½ fresh lemon, juiced

1 tbsp. fresh parsley, finely chopped

½ tsp. Italian seasoning

1 tbsp. drained capers

¼ cup olives, chopped

¼ tsp. smoked paprika, ground

¼ tsp. salt

1 tbsp. olive oil

Preparation:

In a small mixing bowl, combine olive oil, Italian seasoning, capers, olives, smoked paprika, and salt.

Place the rice in a heavy-bottomed pot. Add 1 ½ cup of water and bring it to a boil over medium-high heat. Cook for about 10-15 minutes, or until almost all the liquid has been absorbed.

Add lemon juice and orange juice. Give it a good stir and remove from the heat. Set aside to chill completely.

Transfer the rice to a serving bowl and add tuna and parsley. Drizzle with previously prepared mixture and stir well.

Serve immediately.

Nutritional information per serving: Kcal: 370, Protein: 19.2g, Carbs: 40g, Fats: 15.1g

24. Broccoli Lentil Salad

Ingredients:

2 cups fresh broccoli, chopped

½ cup lentils, soaked overnight

¼ cup spring onions, chopped

2 tbsp. parsley, finely chopped

1 garlic clove, minced

1 tsp. Dijon mustard

1 tsp. maple syrup

1 tbsp. olive oil

1 tbsp. apple cider vinegar

¼ tsp. black pepper

½ salt

Preparation:

Drain the lentils and place in a deep pot. Add two cups of water and bring it to boil. Cook for 20 minutes. Remove from the heat and drain well. Set aside.

Rinse the broccoli under cold running water using a large

colander. Drain and chop into bite-sized pieces. Steam for 10 minutes, or until tender.

In a small mixing bowl, combine parsley, Dijon mustard, maple syrup, olive oil, apple cider vinegar, pepper, and salt. Mix until well combined.

In a large salad bowl, combine lentils and broccoli. Drizzle with previously prepared dressing and give it a good stir.

Serve immediately.

Nutritional information per serving: Kcal: 370, Protein: 19.2g, Carbs: 40g, Fats: 15.1g

25. Sesame Chicken Salad

Ingredients:

4 oz. chicken breast, skinless and boneless

½ small onion, chopped

2 tsp. soy sauce

½ tsp. dried rosemary, ground

½ cup cherry tomatoes, chopped

¼ cup cottage cheese

1 tsp. sesame seeds

1 tsp. balsamic vinegar

2 cups Romaine lettuce, roughly chopped

1 tbsp. olive oil

Salt to taste

Preparation:

Rinse the chicken under running water and pat-dry with a kitchen paper. Transfer to a cutting board and cut into strips. Generously brush with soy sauce and sprinkle with rosemary. Let it sit for 10 minutes to allow spices to penetrate into the meat.

Preheat the oil in a skillet over medium-high heat. Add chicken and cook for 5 minutes, or until golden brown.

In a large salad bowl, combine lettuce, cheese, and cherry tomatoes. Top with meat and sprinkle all with sesame seeds and balsamic vinegar.

Add some salt to taste. However it's optional.

Enjoy!

Nutritional information per serving: Kcal: 371, Protein: 34.7g, Carbs: 14.1g, Fats: 19.9g

26. Beet Salad with Leeks

Ingredients:

2 large beets, chopped into bite-sized pieces

1 cup leeks, chopped

1 large carrot, sliced

1 garlic clove, minced

1 cup Greek yogurt

½ tsp. dried thyme

½ whole lemon, juiced

½ tsp. black pepper

Salt

1 tbsp. olive oil

Preparation:

Rinse the beet well and trim off the green parts. Place it in a deep pot and add water enough to cover. Bring it to a boil and cook for 20 minutes. Remove from the heat and drain. Let it cool completely and chop into bite-sized pieces.

Preheat the oil in a skillet over medium-high heat. Add

carrots and cook for 5 minutes, stirring occasionally. Add leeks and garlic. Pour in some water to help the cooking process. Stir-fry for about 10-15 minutes, or until the leeks are tender.

In a small mixing bowl, combine Greek yogurt, lemon juice, thyme, pepper, and salt. Mix until well combined.

Now, combine cooked beets, carrots, and leeks in a salad bowl. Drizzle over with yogurt dressing and give it a good stir.

Serve immediately.

Nutritional information per serving: Kcal: 332, Protein: 25.8g, Carbs: 49.6g, Fats: 4.8g

27. Sweet Potato Kale Salad with Sesame Seeds

Ingredients:

1 medium-sized sweet potato, chopped

2 cups fresh kale, chopped

1 tsp. apple cider vinegar

1 tsp. avocado oil

1 tsp. sesame seeds

1 garlic clove, minced

Salt and pepper to taste

Preparation:

Peel and wash the potato. Cut into bite-sized pieces and transfer to a large pot. Add water enough to cover and sprinkle with some salt. Bring to a boil over medium-high heat. Cook for 5 minutes and turn off the heat. Cover with a lid and let it stand in hot water.

Using a large colander, rinse the kale under running water. Drain and torn into small pieces.

Preheat the oil in a saucepan over medium-high heat. Add garlic and cook for 2-3 minutes. Now, add kale and continue to cook for 3-4 minutes, or until wilted. Remove from the heat and set aside.

In a large salad bowl, combine sweet potato and kale. Drizzle with apple cider vinegar and sprinkle with sesame seeds. Give it a good stir and serve immediately.

Nutritional information per serving: Kcal: 198, Protein: 7.1g, Carbs: 39.6g, Fats: 2.3g

28. Watercress Mango Salad with Pomegranate Seeds

Ingredients:

2 cups watercress, chopped

1 ripe mango, chopped

¼ cup pomegranate seeds

1 tbsp. walnuts, chopped

1 orange, freshly juiced

½ lemon, freshly juiced

3 tsp. hemp oil

1 tsp. honey

Salt and pepper to taste

Preparation:

Using a large colander, rinse the watercress under cold running water. Drain and set aside.

Peel the mango and chop into bite-sized pieces. Set aside.

In a small mixing bowl, combine orange juice, lemon juice, hemp oil, honey, salt, and pepper. Mix until well combined and set aside.

In a salad bowl, combine watercress and mango. Drizzle with previously prepared dressing and give it a good stir.

Top with pomegranate seeds and walnuts before serving.

Nutritional information per serving: Kcal: 198, Protein: 7.1g, Carbs: 39.6g, Fats: 2.3g

29. Spicy Orange Cumin Salad

Ingredients:

3 large oranges, peeled

1 small red onion, chopped

2 tsp. olive oil

¼ cup olives, pitted

1 whole lime, juiced

½ tsp. black pepper, ground

½ tsp. black cumin powder

Preparation:

Peel the orange and divide into wedges. Set aside.

Peel the onions and cut into thin slices along with olives.

In a small mixing bowl, combine lime juice, pepper, and cumin powder. Mix until well combined. Set aside.

Now, combine orange, onions, and olives in a salad bowl. Drizzle with previously prepared dressing.

Optionally, top with finely chopped coriander leaves or basil.

Serve immediately.

Nutritional information per serving: Kcal: 244, Protein: 3.2g, Carbs: 47.1g, Fats: 6.9g

30. Cauliflower Broccoli Salad with Dried Cranberries

Ingredients:

2 cups cauliflower, chopped

2 cups broccoli, chopped

1 tbsp. dried cranberries

1 tbsp. almond flakes

1 tsp. Dijon mustard

1 whole lemon, juiced

2 garlic cloves, minced

1 tsp. avocado oil

½ tsp. black pepper, ground

½ tsp. salt

Preparation:

Line a small baking sheet with some parchment paper. Spread the almond flakes evenly in one layer. Place it in the oven and bake for 2 minutes at 450 degrees. Remove from the oven and let it cool completely.

Rinse the cauliflower and broccoli using a large colander.

Chop into bite-sized pieces and place in a large bowl. Add cranberries and toasted almonds and set aside.

In a small mixing bowl, combine Dijon mustard, lemon juice, garlic, avocado oil, pepper, and salt. Mix until combined and drizzle the salad. Give it a good stir and serve immediately.

Enjoy!

Nutritional information per serving: Kcal: 291, Protein: 15.1g, Carbs: 29g, Fats: 14.7g

31. Creamy Tuna Tomato Salad

Ingredients:

1 large tomato, chopped

4 oz. canned tuna, drained

1 large green bell pepper, chopped

1 small cucumber, cubed

1 cup Greek yogurt

1 tsp. apple cider vinegar

1 tsp. pine nuts

1 tbsp. extra-virgin olive oil

Salt and pepper to taste

Preparation:

Wash the tomato and chop into bite-sized pieces. Place in a large salad bowl and set aside.

Cut the pepper lengthwise into halves. Remove the stem and seeds. Chop into small pieces and add to the bowl.

Wash the cucumber and cut into small cubes. Add to the bowl and set aside.

Now, combine yogurt, vinegar, pine nuts, and olive oil in a small mixing bowl. Add salt and pepper according to your taste and mix well.

Drizzle the creamy dressing over the salad and give it a good stir. Add more salt and pepper if needed.

Serve immediately.

Nutritional information per serving: Kcal: 309, Protein: 27.7g, Carbs: 17.7g, Fats: 15.1g

32. Grape Tomato Avocado Salad with Greek Dressing

Ingredients:

1 cup grape tomatoes, chopped

1 small cucumber, chopped

½ ripe avocado, chopped

1 small purple onion, sliced

½ cup Feta cheese, crumbled

1 tbsp. fresh parsley, finely chopped

2 tbsp. olive oil

½ whole lemon, juiced

1 tsp. Dijon mustard

1 garlic clove, crushed

1 tsp. fresh basil, finely chopped

¼ tsp. dried oregano, ground

Salt to taste

Preparation:

In a mixing bowl, combine olive oil, fresh lemon juice, Dijon mustard, garlic, fresh basil, oregano, and salt. Mix until well combined and set aside.

Wash cucumber and cut into thin slices. Set aside.

Using a large colander, rinse the grape tomatoes under running water. Drain and cut each in half. Set aside.

Cut the avocado in half. Remove the pit and cut into thin slices. Reserve the rest in the refrigerator. Optionally, sprinkle with some lemon juice and set aside for 5 minutes.

Peel the onion and chop into small pieces.

Now, combine tomatoes, cucumber, avocado, and onion in a salad bowl. Drizzle all with previously prepared dressing and give it a gentle stir. Sprinkle all with fresh parsley and serve immediately.

Nutritional information per serving: Kcal: 253, Protein: 5.8g, Carbs: 12.6g, Fats: 21.5g

33.   Smoked Trout Fusilli Salad

Ingredients:

3 oz. fusilli pasta

2 oz. smoked trout, thinly sliced

½ cup sour cream

2 large red bell peppers, chopped

½ tsp. dried dill, ground

½ whole lemon, juiced

1 tbsp. olive oil

Salt and pepper to taste

Preparation:

Place the pasta in a deep pot and water enough to cover. Bring to a boil over medium-high heat. Cook for 10-13 minutes. Remove from the heat and drain using a large colander. Rinse under cold running water and set aside.

Cut the bell peppers lengthwise into halves. Remove the stems and seeds. Chop into small pieces and set aside.

In a small bowl, combine sour cream, lemon juice, olive oil, salt, and pepper. Mix until well combined.

In a salad bowl, combine pasta, smoked trout, and bell peppers. Drizzle with prepared dressing and gently stir.

Optionally, garnish with some fresh parsley, or add a few olives before serving.

Enjoy!

Nutritional information per serving: Kcal: 288, Protein: 10.8g, Carbs: 29g, Fats: 14.9g

34. Mexican Potato Salad

Ingredients:

2 large potatoes, cut into cubes

1 large red bell pepper, chopped

¼ cup cheddar cheese, shredded

2 tbsp. red wine vinegar

1 tbsp. corn, rinsed and drained

½ cup spring onions, chopped

1 tbsp. fresh parsley, finely chopped

¼ cup Greek yogurt

2 tbsp. olive oil

½ whole lime, juiced

½ tsp. garlic powder

1 tsp. dried oregano, ground

¼ tsp. cumin powder

¼ tsp. chili powder

½ tsp. black pepper, ground

Salt

Preparation:

In a mixing bowl, combine Greek yogurt, olive oil, lime juice, garlic powder, oregano, cumin, chili powder, salt, and pepper. Mix until well combined and refrigerate.

Peel and wash the potatoes. Place in a deep pot and sprinkle with some salt. Add water enough to cover and bring to a boil over medium-high heat. Cook for 20 minutes, or until tender. Remove from the heat and drain. Set aside to cool completely. Chop into bite-sized cubes and set aside.

In a small bowl, combine salt and red wine vinegar. Mix until the salt has been dissolved. Drizzle over the potatoes and give it a good stir and set aside until all the liquid has been soaked up.

Now, add bell peppers and shredded cheddar cheese. Drizzle all with previously prepared yogurt mixture and gently stir.

Serve immediately.

Nutritional information per serving: Kcal: 278, Protein: 8.1g, Carbs: 40.9g, Fats: 10.4g

35. Eggplant Chermoula Salad

Ingredients:

2 medium-sized eggplants, sliced

2 tbsp. olive oil

1 garlic clove, minced

½ tsp. cumin powder

½ tsp. coriander powder

½ tsp. smoked paprika

1 tbsp. fresh parsley, finely chopped

1 tbsp. fresh cilantro, finely chopped

¼ cup fresh spring onions, chopped

1 tbsp. lemon juice, freshly squeezed

Salt

Preparation:

Preheat the oven to 400 degrees. Line some parchment paper over a baking sheet and set aside.

Rinse well the eggplants and pat-dry with a kitchen paper. Transfer to a cutting board and cut into thin slices using a sharp knife.

Spread the eggplant over a prepared baking sheet and bake for 20-25 minutes.

When done, remove from the oven and let it cool completely.

In a food processor, combine olive oil, garlic, cumin powder, coriander powder, smoked paprika, parsley, cilantro, spring onions, fresh lemon juice, and salt. Pulse until well incorporated.

Transfer the chilled eggplant to a serving dish and drizzle over with chermoula dressing.

Optionally, serve with some garlic toasted bread.

Enjoy!

Nutritional information per serving: Kcal: 269, Protein: 6g, Carbs: 34.5g, Fats: 15.3g

36. Zucchini Carpaccio Salad

Ingredients:

3 medium-sized zucchinis, thinly sliced

¼ cup Parmesan cheese, thinly sliced

2 tbsp. capers, drained

¼ cup black olives

1 whole lemon, freshly juiced

½ cup fresh mint, roughly chopped

3 tbsp. olive oil

1 tsp. apple cider vinegar

Salt and pepper to taste

Preparation:

Rinse and pat-dry the zucchinis. Using a sharp paring knife, cut thin lengthwise slices. Discard the middle parts with seeds.

Spread the zucchini slices in one layer over a large baking sheet. Sprinkle with salt, pepper, and vinegar. Set aside for 30 minutes.

Now, in a small mixing bowl, combine olive oil, lemon juice, salt, and pepper. Mix until well combined.

Transfer the zucchini to a serving bowl and drizzle with previously prepared dressing. Top with mint, capers, and cheese.

Stir once and serve immediately.

Enjoy!

Nutritional information per serving: Kcal: 304, Protein: 9.2g, Carbs: 13.8g, Fats: 26.6g

37. Roquefort Radish Salad with Raspberries

Ingredients:

2 cups fresh arugula, chopped

3 medium-sized radishes, sliced

½ cup Roquefort cheese, (or any other blue cheese you have on hand)

½ cup fresh raspberries

1 tbsp. walnuts, finely chopped

1 tbsp. olive oil

1 tsp. apple cider vinegar

¼ tsp. dried dill, ground

Salt and pepper

Preparation:

Using a large colander, rinse the arugula under cold running water. Drain and roughly torn with your hands. Transfer to a large salad bowl and set aside. Optionally, sprinkle with some lemon juice for some extra flavor.

Rinse the radishes and trim off the green parts. Cut into thin slices and add to the bowl with arugula.

Cut the cheese into small cubes and add to the salad.

Now, sprinkle all with olive oil, apple cider vinegar, dried dill, and salt. Give it a good stir and top with raspberries and walnuts.

Serve immediately.

Nutritional information per serving: Kcal: 226, Protein: 9.1g, Carbs: 5.8g, Fats: 19.3g

38. Asparagus Strawberry Salad

Ingredients:

5 oz. asparagus, trimmed and chopped

6 oz. strawberries, chopped

¼ cup raspberries

1 tbsp. balsamic vinegar

1 tbsp. olive oil

Salt and pepper

Preparation:

In a food processor, combine raspberries, balsamic vinegar, olive oil, salt, and pepper. Pulse until smooth and set aside.

Rinse and drain the asparagus. Trim off the woody ends and cut into bite-sized pieces. Transfer to a deep pot and add enough water to cover. Bring to a boil over medium-high heat. Cook for 2 minutes and remove from the heat. Drain and set aside to cool completely.

Using a large colander, rinse well the strawberries. Drain and remove the stems. Chop into bite-sized pieces.

Now, combine asparagus and strawberries in a large bowl.

Drizzle with previously prepared sauce and give it a good stir.

Serve immediately.

Nutritional information per serving: Kcal: 222, Protein: 4.6g, Carbs: 22.4g, Fats: 14.9g

39. Creamy Cucumber Salad

Ingredients:

2 cups Greek yogurt

2 medium-sized cucumbers, finely chopped

2 garlic cloves, minced

¼ cup fresh dill, finely chopped

2 tbsp. extra-virgin olive oil

1 tbsp. walnuts, finely chopped

Salt and pepper to taste

Preparation:

Wash the cucumbers and chop into small pieces. Place in a large salad bowl and set aside.

In a small bowl, garlic, fresh dill, olive oil, salt, and pepper. Mix until well incorporated and pour over the cucumbers. Mix once and set aside for 15 minutes to allow flavors to merge.

Now, add Greek yogurt and stir until all well combined. Top with walnuts before serving.

Optionally, add some cayenne pepper or chili for some

extra flavor.

Enjoy!

Nutritional information per serving: Kcal: 360, Protein: 24.5g, Carbs: 23.7g, Fats: 20.9g

40. Greek Lentil Salad

Ingredients:

½ cup lentils, soaked overnight

1 small purple onion, chopped

1 small cucumber, chopped

½ cup cherry tomatoes, halved

¼ cup Kalamata olives

¼ cup Feta cheese, cubed

1 tsp. fresh dill, finely chopped

2 tbsp. olive oil

1 garlic clove, crushed

¼ tsp. dried oregano, ground

1 tbsp. lemon juice, freshly squeezed

Salt and pepper to taste

Preparation:

In a small mixing bowl, combine olive oil, garlic, dried oregano, lemon juice, salt, and pepper. Mix until well combined and set aside.

Drain the lentils and place in a deep pot. Add 2 cups of water and a pinch of salt. Bring to a boil over medium-high heat. Cook for 20 minutes and remove from the heat. Drain well and rinse under cold water to chill. Set aside.

Wash and prepare the vegetables.

In a large salad bowl, combine onions, cucumber, cherry tomatoes, Kalamata olives, and Feta cheese. Add lentils and stir once.

Now, drizzle with previously prepared dressing and stir well.

Serve immediately.

Nutritional information per serving: Kcal: 273, Protein: 11.5g, Carbs: 28.1g, Fats: 13.8g

41.   Broccoli Salad with Raisins

Ingredients:

2 cups broccoli, chopped

1 small purple onion, finely chopped

1 tbsp. raisins

½ cup cheddar cheese, cut into cubes

½ cup cherry tomatoes, halved

2 tsp. apple cider vinegar

1 tbsp. olive oil

Salt and pepper

Preparation:

Using a large colander, rinse the broccoli under cold running water. Chop into bite-sized pieces and set aside.

Peel the onion and finely chop. Set aside.

Rinse the cherry tomatoes and remove the stems. Cut each tomato in half and set aside. In case you use the regular tomato, remove the seeds and cut into small pieces.

Now, combine broccoli, onion, tomatoes, raisins, and

cheddar cheese in a large salad bowl. Sprinkle all with apple cider vinegar, olive oil, salt, and pepper.

Mix until all well incorporated and serve immediately.

Nutritional information per serving: Kcal: 242, Protein: 10.5g, Carbs: 15.1g, Fats: 16.8g

42.   Classic Waldorf Salad

Ingredients:

2 large Granny Smith's apple, cored

2 large celery sticks

1 cup Greek yogurt

½ whole lemon, juiced

1 tbsp. walnuts, minced

Salt and pepper to taste

Parsley

Preparation:

Wash the apples and cut lengthwise in half. Remove the core and cut into thin slices or strips. Set aside.

Rinse the celery and discard the leaves. Cut each stick into 1-inch thick strips. Set aside.

In a mixing bowl, combine Greek yogurt, lemon, salt, and pepper. Mix until well incorporated and set aside.

Now, combine apples and celery in a salad bowl. Add yogurt mixture and stir until all well combined.

Top with walnuts and garnish with parsley.

Enjoy!

Nutritional information per serving: Kcal: 226, Protein: 11.6g, Carbs: 37.2g, Fats: 4.7g

43. Green Bean Fusilli Salad

Ingredients:

4 oz. fusilli pasta

1 cup green beans

¼ cup Feta cheese, crumbled

¼ cup olives, pitted and chopped

2 garlic cloves, minced

½ onion, finely chopped

1 cup yogurt, low-fat

1 tsp. yellow mustard

2 tbsp. olive oil

½ tsp. dried dill, ground

½ tsp. red pepper, ground

Salt

Preparation:

Place the pasta in a deep pot. Add enough water to cover and bring it to a boil. Sprinkle with some salt and cook for 10 minutes over medium-high heat. Remove from the heat and transfer to a large colander. Rinse under cold running water and set aside.

Place the green beans in a deep pot and cover with water. Bring to a boil over medium-high heat and cook for 5 minutes. Remove from the heat and drain. Set aside.

Preheat one tablespoon of olive oil in a large skillet over medium-high heat. Add onions and garlic. Stir-fry for 2-3 minutes, or until translucent. Add green beans and cook for 5 minutes. Remove from the heat and transfer to a large salad bowl.

Add pasta to the bowl and stir well. Set aside.

Now, combine the remaining olive oil, yogurt, mustard, dried dill, red pepper, and a pinch of salt in a mixing bowl. Mix until well combined and pour over prepared beans and pasta. Top with olives and cheese before serving.

Enjoy!

Nutritional information per serving: Kcal: 264, Protein: 9.3g, Carbs: 31.5g, Fats: 11.2g

44. Cooked Celery Salad

Ingredients:

4 celery sticks, with leaves

1 whole lemon, juiced

3 tbsp. walnuts, halved

1 small purple onion, finely chopped

2 tbsp. white wine vinegar

2 cups lamb's lettuce, roughly chopped

1 tsp. flaxseed oil

½ tsp. salt

½ tsp. black pepper, ground

Preparation:

Rinse the celery under cold running water and drain. Transfer to a cutting board and separate sticks and leaves. Chop the sticks into strips and finely chop the leaves. Set aside.

Transfer the celery sticks in a deep pot. Cover with water and bring to a boil over medium-high heat. Cook for 8 minutes. Add celery leaves and fresh lemon juice. Stir once and cook for 2-3 minutes more. Remove from the heat and drain. Rinse all under cold running water immediately. Set aside.

In a mixing bowl, combine onions, vinegar, salt, and pepper. Mix until well incorporated. Add flaxseed oil and mix again until combined.

Now, arrange the lamb's lettuce over a serving dish and top with celery. Drizzle with previously prepared dressing.

Serve cold.

Nutritional information per serving: Kcal: 273, Protein: 8.8g, Carbs: 17.9g, Fats: 19g

45. Avocado Egg Salad

Ingredients:

1 ripe avocado, cut into cubes

2 large eggs, hard-boiled

2 spring onions, chopped

½ cup Greek yogurt

1 tbsp. sour cream

1 whole lime, juiced

1 tsp. fresh thyme, finely chopped

Salt and pepper to taste

Preparation:

Place the eggs in a deep pot. Add water enough to cover and bring to a boil over medium-high heat. Cook for 10-12 minutes. Remove from the heat and transfer to a bowl with ice cold water. You can add a few ice cubes to speed up the process. Peel and cut into bite-sized pieces. Set aside.

Peel the avocado and cut lengthwise in half. Remove the pit and cut into bite-sized cubes. Set aside.

In a mixing bowl, combine Greek yogurt, sour cream, lime

juice, thyme, salt, and pepper. Mix until combined.

In a serving bowl, combine eggs and avocado. Drizzle with previously prepared dressing and give it a good stir.

Serve immediately.

Nutritional information per serving: Kcal: 343, Protein: 14g, Carbs: 16.3g, Fats: 27g

46. Grilled Mustard Turkey Salad

Ingredients:

8 oz. turkey breast, skinless and boneless

1 tbsp. yellow mustard

3 tsp. olive oil

½ tsp. salt

½ tsp. black pepper, ground

2 cups Romaine lettuce, chopped

1 cup lamb's lettuce

½ cup cherry tomatoes, chopped

1 tbsp. Parmesan cheese, shredded

2 tsp. red wine vinegar

Preparation:

Rinse and drain the turkey breast. Transfer to a cutting board and cut into thin slices. Set aside.

In a small mixing bowl, combine 2 teaspoons of olive oil, salt, black pepper, and mustard. Mix until combined and pour over the meat. Rub with your hands to allow flavors to penetrate into the meat. Cover the dish with a plastic foil and refrigerate for 1 hour.

Preheat the grill to medium-high. Add meat and grill for 3-4 minutes on each side. Remove from the heat and transfer to a cutting board. Let it chill for a while and then cut into strips.

Wash and prepare the vegetables.

In a large salad bowl, combine lettuce, lamb's lettuce, and cherry tomatoes. Top with turkey strips and drizzle with red wine vinegar. Sprinkle with parmesan cheese and serve immediately.

Nutritional information per serving: Kcal: 248, Protein: 25g, Carbs: 9.6g, Fats: 12.4g

47. Shrimp Avocado Salad

Ingredients:

4 oz. shrimps, cleaned and deveined

½ ripe avocado, chopped

¼ cup Feta cheese, crumbled

1 medium-sized green bell pepper, chopped

½ cup cherry tomatoes, chopped

½ cup fresh mint, roughly chopped

1 small purple onion, chopped

¼ cup green olives, pitted

1 tbsp. fresh parsley, finely chopped

1 whole lime, juiced

¼ tsp. garlic powder

¼ tsp. dried oregano, ground

½ tsp. red pepper flakes

2 tbsp. olive oil

Salt to taste

Preparation:

In a small mixing bowl, combine lime juice, oregano, garlic, 1 tablespoon of olive oil, pepper flakes, and salt. Mix until well combined and set aside.

Wash and prepare the vegetables.

In a large salad bowl, combine cherry tomatoes, mint, purple onion, green olives, and parsley. Drizzle with previously prepared dressing and refrigerate for 20 minutes.

Preheat the remaining oil in a skillet over medium-high heat. Add shrimps and sprinkle with some salt and red pepper. Cook for 2-3 minutes, or until set. Remove from the heat and set aside to chill for a while.

Now, add cheese and avocado to the salad. Mix again and top with shrimps. Garnish with fresh mint and serve immediately.

Enjoy!

Nutritional information per serving: Kcal: 264, Protein: 12.6g, Carbs: 12.2g, Fats: 19.6g

MEAL RECIPES

1. Super Broccoli Power

Description:

Broccoli is very rich in vitamins K, C, and calcium, which is known for its bone-building benefits.

Ingredients:

- 2 cups broccoli florets
- 1 yellow bell pepper, sliced
- 2 teaspoons chili powder
- 1 teaspoon garlic powder
- salt and pepper to taste
- 1 tablespoon extra-virgin olive oil

How to prepare:

- Preheat an oven to 400 degrees F (200 degrees C).
- Combine the broccoli and bell pepper in a bowl. Sprinkle, chili powder, garlic powder, salt, and pepper over the vegetables; drizzle with the olive oil and toss to coat. Spread the vegetables into a shallow baking dish.
- Bake in the preheated oven until the vegetables

are tender and beginning to brown, 15 to 20 minutes.

Nutritional facts:

Calories: 69kcal, Fat: 3.9g, Carbs: 8g, Protein: 2.1g, Sodium: 815mg

2. Crunchy Eggplant Delight

Description:

Nightshade vegetables, including eggplant, are disease-fighting powerhouses that give the maximum nutrition for a small number of calories.

Ingredients:

- eggplant, sliced into strips
- 1/2 cup soft bread crumbs
- 1/8 cup grated Romano cheese
- 1 clove garlic, chopped
- 2 sprigs fresh parsley, chopped
- 1/2 teaspoon dried oregano
- salt and pepper to taste

How to prepare:

- Preheat oven to 400 degrees F (200 degrees C).
- Cut eggplant strips in half. Lay strips on a baking sheet.
- In a small bowl combine bread crumbs, Romano cheese, garlic, parsley, oregano, salt and pepper. Sprinkle over eggplant strips and drizzle with oil.
- Bake in preheated oven for 25 minutes

Nutritional facts:

Calories: 169kcal, Fat: 8.9g, Carbs: 19g, Sodium: 155mg

3. Healthberries

Description:

Recent clinical studies have shown that diets containing an abundance of flavonoids (a broad class of plant pigments) are associated with reduced levels of inflammation. These natural compounds are found especially in strawberries

Ingredients:

- 2 bunches spinach
- 4 cups sliced strawberries
- 1/2 cup vegetable oil
- 1/4 cup white wine vinegar
- 1/2 cup white sugar
- 1/4 teaspoon paprika
- 2 tablespoons sesame seeds
- 1 tablespoon poppy seeds

How to prepare:

- In a large bowl, toss together the spinach and strawberries.
- Whisk together the oil, vinegar, sugar, paprika, sesame seeds, and poppy seeds. Pour over the spinach and strawberries.

Nutritional facts:

Calories: 255kcal, Fat: 16g, Carbs: 22.8g, Sodium: 69mg

4. Lemon Broccolini

Description:

A broccoli lovers delight with a sweet-and-sour taste! Broccoli is abundant in vitamin K, which in high amounts may slow the progression of osteoarthritis.

Ingredients:

- 1 head fresh broccoli, cut into florets
- 1 tablespoon olive oil
- 2 tablespoons lemon juice
- 1 teaspoon lemon zest
- 1/4 cup blanched slivered almonds

How to prepare:

- Steam or boil broccoli until tender, approximately 4 to 8 minutes. Drain.
- In a small saucepan, melt olive oil over medium low heat. Remove from heat.
- Stir in lemon juice. lemon zest, and almonds. Pour over hot broccoli, and serve.

Nutritional facts:

Calories: 170 kcal, Fat: 15.2g, Carbs: 7g, Protein: 3.7g, Sodium: 107mg, Cholesterol: 31mg

5. Easy Flave Apples

Description:

Research suggests that eating some apple on a daily basis might lower levels of cholesterol, a key marker of inflammation in the blood. "An apple a day keeps the doctor away".

Ingredients:

- 2 apples, diced
- 1 teaspoon white sugar
- 1/2 teaspoon ground cinnamon

How to prepare:

- Place apples in a microwave-safe bowl; heat in microwave for 30 seconds. Sprinkle sugar and cinnamon over apples and stir to coat.
- Heat apples into the microwave until soft and warm, about 1 minute more.

Nutritional facts:

Calories: 255kcal, Fat: 16g, Carbs: 22.8g, Sodium: 69mg

6. Lemon Trout

Description:

One way to calm inflammation is with medicine your doctor prescribes. Another way is to add a few key anti-inflammatory foods to your diet. Among the most potent edible inflammation fighters are essential fatty acids called omega-3s – particularly the kinds of fatty acids found in trout.

Ingredients:

- 4 cups all-purpose flour
- 2 tablespoons lemon pepper
- 1/2 tablespoon salt
- 1/2 teaspoon dried thyme
- 1/2 teaspoon cayenne pepper
- 1 teaspoon onion powder
- 1/4 cup grated lemon zest, divided
- 4 (6 ounce) fillets rainbow trout
- 1 lemon cut in wedges
- 1/2 cup lemon juice
- 1/2 cup extra-virgin olive oil

How to prepare:

- In a large bowl, stir together the flour, lemon

pepper, salt, thyme, cayenne and half of the lemon zest. Combine the lemon juice and remaining lemon zest in a shallow dish and soak fish fillets for about 1 minute.
- Heat oil in a large skillet over medium heat. Dip the trout fillets in the flour mixture so that both sides are coated. Shake off the excess and place fillets in the hot oil. Cook for 3 to 4 minutes on each side, until golden brown and fish can be flaked with a fork. Discard the leftover lemon juice.

Nutritional facts:

Calories: 979kcal, Fat: 40g, Carbs: 103g, Protein: 48.6g, Sodium: 2500mg

7. Salmons 'N' Lemons

Description:

Salmon helps reduce joint pain and stiffness as well as signs of inflammation in people with rheumatoid arthritis.

Ingredients:

- 1 (16 ounce) red salmon, drained and flaked
- 1 lemon, juiced
- 1/2 cup organic raisins
- 1 apple, cored and minced
- 1 1/2 stalks celery, chopped fine
- 1/3 cup mayonnaise, or to taste
- 1/4 teaspoon crushed red pepper flakes

How to prepare:

- Combine red salmon and lemon juice in a glass bowl; mix well.
- Stir in golden raisins, apple, celery, mayonnaise, and crushed red pepper flakes; mix thoroughly.

Nutritional facts:

Calories: 368kcal, Fat: 20.9g, Carbs: 21.2g, Protein: 25g, Sodium: 664mg

8. Salmon Asparagus Security

Description:

One cup of asparagus contains only 24 calories. It's also an excellent source of potassium, vitamin K, folic acid, vitamin C and A, riboflavin, thiamin, and vitamin B6.

Ingredients:

- 1 pound fresh asparagus, trimmed and cut into 1 inch pieces
- 1/2 cup pecans, broken into pieces
- 2 heads red leaf lettuce, rinsed and torn
- 1/2 cup green peas, thawed
- 1/4 pound organic smoked salmon, cut into 1 inch chunks
- 1/4 cup olive oil
- 2 tablespoons lemon juice
- 1 teaspoon Dijon mustard
- 1/2 teaspoon salt
- 1/4 teaspoon pepper

How to prepare:

- Bring a pot of water to a boil. Place asparagus in the pot, and cook 5 minutes, just until tender. Drain, and set aside.

- Place the pecans in a skillet over medium heat. Cook 5 minutes, stirring frequently, until lightly toasted.
- In a large bowl, toss together the asparagus, pecans, red leaf lettuce, peas, and salmon.
- In a separate bowl, mix the olive oil, lemon juice, Dijon mustard, salt, and pepper. Toss with the salad or serve on the side.

Nutritional facts:

Calories: 159kcal, Fat: 12.9g, Carbs: 7g, Protein: 6g, Sodium: 304mg

9. Canadian Style Salmon

Description:

Eating salmon once a week reduces risk of rheumatoid arthritis by half.

Ingredients:

- 1/4 cup maple syrup
- 1 tablespoon olive oil
- 1 clove garlic, minced
- 1/4 teaspoon garlic salt
- 1/8 teaspoon ground black pepper
- 1 pound salmon

How to prepare:

- In a small bowl, mix the maple syrup, garlic, garlic salt, and pepper.
- Place salmon in a shallow glass baking dish, and coat with the maple syrup mixture. Cover the dish, and marinate salmon in the refrigerator 30 minutes, turning once.
- Preheat oven to 400 degrees F (200 degrees C).
- Place the baking dish in the preheated oven, and bake salmon uncovered 20 minutes, or until easily flaked with a fork.

Nutritional facts:

Calories: 265kcal, Fat: 12g, Carbs: 14g, Protein: 23g, Sodium: 633mg

10. Neat Salmon

Description:

Quick, healthy dinner option. Low-calorie for weight loss. Wild-caught Sockeye salmon is a super food because of its omega-3 fatty acid content. Easy recipe for adding more Omega-3 EFAs in your diet.

Ingredients:

- 1 pound Wild-caught Salmon, cut into 4 filets
- 2 oranges, thinly sliced
- 3/4C fresh squeezed orange juice
- 2T fresh squeezed lime juice
- 2T virgin, unrefined coconut oil, melted or olive oil
- 1t lemon zest – dried or 1T fresh lemon zest
- 1T coconut or palm sugar or use raw honey or pure maple syrup
- coarsely ground salt
- 1/4t chipotle pepper or cayenne pepper or chili powder

How to prepare:

- Preheat oven to 450º. Slice two oranges into very thin slices, discard ends, and set aside.
- Squeeze orange and lime with a citrus juicer.

Measure out 1/4 cup fresh orange juice and 2 tablespoons fresh lime juice and add to a small glass bowl along with the lemon zest. Whisk in melted coconut oil or olive oil and sweetener of choice, along with salt and pepper.

- Line a baking sheet with parchment paper. Using a basting brush, brush one side of each of the salmon filets with the citrus mixture then arrange filets on top of parchment paper. Brush tops of salmon with the citrus mixture.

Nutritional facts:

Calories: 275, Fat: 18g, Carbs: 20g, Protein: 23g, Sodium: 215mg

11. Drunken Grapefruit Salad

Description:

Grapefruit is well known for its beneficial effects in patients with rheumatoid arthritis. Daily consumption of grapefruit has been associated with lowering of inflammation caused due to inflammatory diseases .

Ingredients:

- 8 cups refrigerated grapefruit, drained and juice reserved
- 1/4 cup white sugar
- 3 fluid ounces gin
- 8 leaves fresh mint, minced

How to prepare:

- Mix grapefruit, 1/2 cup reserved juice, and sugar in a bowl until sugar dissolves. Transfer grapefruit mixture to 8 serving cups; top each with about 1 teaspoon gin. Sprinkle minced mint over each cup. Garnish each cup with 1 mint leaf.

Nutritional facts:

Calories: 139kcal, Fat: 0.2g, Carbs: 28.6g, Protein: 1.4g, Sodium: 5mg

12. Grapefruit and its Friends

Description:

Grapefruit can be called as one of the Nature's medicine due to its tremendous health benefits. It is known to be beneficial for boosting the immune system. It is juicy, tangy and tart in taste and is known for its numerous health benefits. It is rich in antioxidants and various vitamins like Vitamin C, Vitamin A, Vitamin K, Vitamin D and Vitamin B complex.

Ingredients:

- 2 pink grapefruit, peeled and sectioned
- 1 large ripe avocado - peeled, pitted, and diced
- 1 cup alfalfa sprouts
- 1 lemon, juiced
- 3 tablespoons olive oil
- 1 pinch salt
- 1 pinch ground black pepper

How to prepare:

- Create 4 small salads with the fruits used
- Mix lemon juice, olive oil, salt, and black pepper in a small bowl; drizzle dressing over each salad.

Nutritional facts:

Calories: 277kcal, Fat: 20.7g, Carbs: 25.1g, Protein: 3.8g, Sodium: 7mg

13. Arthitis Buster

Description:

The rich, creamy texture of avocados come in part from its high content of anti-inflammatory monounsaturated fat. Avocados are also rich in the carotenoid lutein. Unlike most fruits, avocados are a good source of vitamin E, a micronutrient with anti-inflammatory effects. Diets high in these compounds are linked to decreased risk of the joint damage seen in early osteoarthritis.

Ingredients:

- 1 avocado
- 1/2 teaspoon minced garlic
- 1/2 teaspoon minced fresh ginger root
- 1 tablespoon olive oil

How to prepare:

- Stir together garlic, ginger, and olive oil; set aside for five minutes to allow the flavors to blend.
- Cut the avocado in half, and discard the pit; divide the sauce between the avocado halves.

Nutritional facts:

Calories: 164kcal, Fat: 15g, Carbs: 9.1g, Protein: 2.2g,

Sodium: 157mg

14.   Fresh Summer Organic Salsa

Description:

Avocados contain more than 25 vitamins, minerals, and phytonutrients. They have fiber, potassium, vitamin E, B-vitamins, and folic acid. Avocados are considered an excellent source of healthy fats when combined with a calorie-wise diet.

Ingredients:

- 2 tbsp organic olive oil
- 1 tbsp fresh lime juice
- 1/4 cup chopped cilantro
- 1/4 tsp unrefined sea salt
- 1/4 tsp freshly ground pepper
- 2 cups fresh organic corn, cut off the cob
- 2 avocados diced into 1/2 pieces
- 2 cups cherry tomatoes, quartered
- 1/4-1/2 cup finely diced red onion

How to prepare:

- In a large bowl, whisk together the olive oil, lime juice, cilantro, salt and pepper.
- Add to it the corn, avocado, cherry tomatoes and red onion.

- Stir gently and serve at room temperature.

Nutritional facts:

Calories: 206.2kcal, Fat: 15.1g, Carbs: 18.9g, Protein: 3.6g

15. Big Bang Fruit

Description:

Strawberries are naturally low in sugar and have more vitamin C per serving than an orange. Vitamin C can lower risk for gout, high blood pressure and cholesterol problems. Research has also shown that women who ate 16 or more strawberries a week had lower C-reactive protein (CRP), a measure of body-wide inflammation linked to arthritis flares and heart disease.

Ingredients:

- 2 avocados peeled and pitted chopped
- 1 cup strawberries finely chopped
- ½ of jalapeno minced, seeds removed
- 2 tbsp chopped cilantro
- ¼ tsp ground cinnamon
- 1 tbsp organic olive oil
- lime juice from ½ of a lime
- ¼ tsp unrefined sea salt

How to prepare:

- Mix all the ingredients together and gently stir.

Nutritional facts:

Calories: 226.8kcal, Fat: 18.8g, Carbs: 15.4g, Protein: 3.7g

16. Veggie Noodles

Description:

This pad Thai recipe is almost easier than calling for take-out. It's so fast and delicious. This meal would provide an excellent source of vitamins and nutrients.

Ingredients:

- 2 zucchini
- 1 carrot
- 2 green onion
- 1/2 cup mushrooms
- 1/2 cup cauliflower
- 1/2 cup mung bean sprouts
- 2 tablespoons sesame oil
- 1 tablespoon lemon juice
- 1 t garlic
- 1 t ginger

How to prepare:

- Use a spiralizer (or mandoline, or peeler) to create your noodles. Add in veggies of your choice then top with the sauce. It tastes even better after it sits to soak the flavors the next day.

Nutritional facts:

Calories: 369kcal, Fat: 14.4g, Carbs: 208g, Protein: 7.1g, Sodium: 957mg

17. Juicy Avocado

Description:

Avocados are thought to be effective at reducing pain and inflammation in people who suffer from osteoarthritis and gout.

Ingredients:

- 1 avocado - peeled, pitted and diced
- 1 lime, juiced
- 1 mango - peeled, seeded and diced
- 1 small red onion, chopped
- 1 habanero pepper, seeded and chopped
- 1 tablespoon chopped fresh cilantro

How to prepare:

- Place the avocado in a serving bowl, and mix with the lime juice.
- Mix in the mango, onion, habanero pepper, cilantro and salt.

Nutritional facts:

Calories: 252kcal, Fat: 15g, Carbs: 33g, Protein: 3g, Sodium: 204mg

18. Early Morning Salad

Description:

A simple spinach salad special by adding avocado, spices and fresh cilantro. Make it ahead, refrigerate and then toss right before serving.

Ingredients:

- 3 tablespoons fresh lime juice
- 3 tablespoons olive oil
- 1 tablespoon chopped fresh cilantro
- 1 teaspoon sugar
- 1/4 teaspoon ground cumin
- 1/4 teaspoon kosher salt
- 1/8 teaspoon black pepper
- 1 Hass avocado, peeled, pitted and thinly sliced
- 1 small red onion, thinly sliced
- 11 ounces baby spinach

How to prepare:

- Whisk lime juice, oil, cilantro, sugar, cumin, salt and pepper in a large serving bowl.
- Stir in avocado and red onion.
- Lay spinach on top. (Salad can be prepared and refrigerated up to 2 hours ahead.) Toss just before

serving.

Nutritional facts:

Calories: 99kcal, Fat: 9g, Carbs: 5g, Sodium: 93mg

19. Garbanzos Soup

Description:

Whole grains lower levels of C-reactive protein (CRP) in the blood. CRP is a marker of inflammation associated with heart disease, diabetes and rheumatoid arthritis. Foods like oatmeal, brown rice and whole-grain cereals are excellent sources of whole grains.

Ingredients:

- 3 tablespoons olive oil
- 1 cup oats
- 5 large tomatoes, halved and sliced
- 1/3 cup onion, chopped
- 1 clove garlic, chopped
- 3 cups water, divided
- 1/2 bunch fresh cilantro
- 2 teaspoons chicken bouillon granules
- 1/2 teaspoon salt

How to prepare:

- Heat a large deep skillet or oven over medium-low heat. Pour in the olive oil, and let it heat up. Add the oats; cook and stir until toasted.
- In a blender or large food processor, combine the

tomatoes, onion, garlic, 1 cup of water, and cilantro. Blend until smooth. Pour into the pan with the toasted oats. Stir in the remaining 2 cups of water, and bring to a boil. Mix in the salt and chicken bouillon. Cover, and simmer for 15 minutes. Enjoy hot or warm.

Nutritional facts:

Calories: 218kcal, Fat: 12.1g, Carbs: 24.6g, Protein: 5.2g, Sodium: 493mg

20. Organic Guacamole

Description:

Avocados are the main ingredient in guacamole, a popular and healthy food commonly used as a sauce, spread or dip.

Ingredients:

- 2 avocados halved, pitted, and removed from peel
- ½ tsp salt
- ¼ tsp pepper
- ¼ cup fresh tomatoes, diced up
- ½ of a lime, juice squeezed out, about 1 tbsp
- 2 tbsp fresh cilantro, chopped
- 1 tbsp red onion (optional)

How to prepare:

- Combine all ingredients and mash with fork.
- Serve immediately.

Nutritional facts:

Calories: 148.9kcal, Fat: 13.4g, Carbs: 8.5g, Protein: 1.8g

21. Banana Oat Energy Bars

Description:

Bananas are simply a great food to consume overall, but especially if you're trying to do something about your arthritis. This vitamin mix includes folate, Vitamin C, and Vitamin B6, all of which help to battle back arthritis and keep your symptoms to a minimum.

Ingredients:

- 2 cups rolled oats
- 2 bananas, mashed
- 2 carrots, grated
- 1 apple, grated
- 1 cup unsweetened applesauce
- 1/2 cup chopped peanuts

How to prepare:

- Preheat oven to 350 degrees F (175 degrees C). Grease a 9x13-inch baking dish.
- Mix oats, bananas, carrots, apple, applesauce, and peanuts together in a bowl; spread into the prepared baking dish.
- Bake in the preheated oven until golden brown, about 20 minutes.

Nutritional facts:

Calories: 124kcal, Fat: 4g, Carbs: 20g, Protein: 3.6g, Sodium: 10mg

22. Breakfast Banana Green Smoothie

Description:

This smoothie is packed with nutrients and vitamins. It's also perfect if you're in a hurry to get to work. For people with arthritis, consuming a banana a day will not necessarily keep the doctor away, but it just might help minimize some of the severe symptoms of this potentially debilitating disease.

Ingredients:

- 2 cups baby spinach leaves, or to taste
- 1 banana
- 1 carrot, peeled and cut into large chunks
- 3/4 cup plain fat-free Greek yogurt, or to taste
- 3/4 cup ice

How to prepare:

- Put spinach, banana, carrot, yogurt, ice, and honey in a blender; blend until smooth.

Nutritional facts:

Calories: 367kcal, Fat: 0.8g, Carbs: 77.4g, Protein: 18.6g, Sodium: 168mg

23. Infused Olive Oil

Description:

Extra-virgin olive oil has benefits beyond stemming inflammation. Several studies have shown benefits for heart health, bone loss and neurological diseases.

Ingredients:

- 2 cups olive oil
- 1 teaspoon coarsely ground black pepper
- 1 tablespoon chopped fresh basil
- 1/2 teaspoon coarse sea salt
- 1 pinch crushed red pepper

How to prepare:

- In a medium bowl, mix together olive oil, coarsely ground black pepper, basil, coarse sea salt and red pepper. Cover and refrigerate the mixture. Allow it to sit approximately 1 hour before serving.

Nutritional facts:

Calories: 239kcal, Fat: 27g, Carbs: 0.1g, Sodium: 56mg

24. Happy Pistachos

Description:

Snack on pistachios to help with weight loss. Pistachios can also help lower LDL cholesterol and are high in potassium and antioxidants, including vitamins A and E and lutein – a compound also found in dark, leafy vegetables.

Ingredients:

- 2 cups shelled pistachios

How to prepare:

- Preheat oven to 350 degrees F.
- Spread the pistachios evenly on a rimmed cookie sheet. Place in the oven for about 6 to 8 minutes They will become very fragrant when they are done.
- Remove from oven and transfer to a plate immediately.
- If you want to remove the skins from the pistachios place them on a clean towel and rub them. The pieces will slide right off. It's easiest to do this when the pistachios are warm.
- Let the pistachios cool and then you can store them.

- They taste amazing in baking recipes when they are toasted.

Nutritional facts:

Calories: 170kcal, Fat: 14g, Carbs: 8g, Protein: 6g

25. Rosemary Walnuts

Description:

With their high ALA content, walnuts head the nut pack in omega-3 content, and researchers studying their effects have found they lower C-reactive protein (CRP), a marker of inflammation linked to increased risk of cardiovascular disease and arthritis. Eating walnuts regularly can lower cholesterol and reduce blood pressure.

Ingredients:

- 2 cups walnuts
- 2 cloves garlic, minced
- 1 tablespoon honey
- 1 tablespoon extra-virgin olive oil
- 1 tablespoon minced fresh rosemary
- 1 teaspoon salt

How to prepare:

- Preheat oven to 350 degrees F (175 degrees C). Line a baking sheet with parchment paper.
- Mix walnuts, garlic, honey, olive oil, rosemary, and salt together in a bowl until walnuts are coated; spread onto the prepared baking sheet.
- Bake in the preheated oven until walnuts are

lightly browned, about 10 minutes.

Nutritional facts:

Calories: 188kcal, Fat: 8g, Carbs: 5.9g, Protein: 3.9g, Sodium: 291mg

26. Roasted Peanuts

Description:

Technically a legume, peanuts are the "nut" with the most protein. They're also cheaper than most nuts, so for people with arthritis trying to managing their weight, for example, they make a filling, inexpensive snack. Peanuts are also a good source of monounsaturated and polyunsaturated fats, and research shows adding them to your diet can help lower "bad" low-density lipoprotein (LDL) cholesterol and reduce heart disease risk. Peanuts deliver about 12% of your daily magnesium requirement, and may help keep blood sugar under control.

Ingredients:

- 1 pound raw peanuts, in shells

How to prepare:

- Preheat oven to 500 degrees F (260 degrees C).
- Arrange peanuts in a single layer on a cookie sheet, and place in the preheated oven.
- Turn oven off. Leave peanuts in oven for 1 hour without opening door. Serve warm or at room temperature.

Nutritional facts:

Calories: 322kcal, Fat: 27.9g, Carbs: 9.2g, Protein: 14.6g, Sodium: 10mg

27. Almond Carrots

Description:

Almonds are a good source of antioxidant vitamin E. Research suggests the monounsaturated fats from an almond-rich diet lower some markers of inflammation.

Ingredients:

- 2 pounds carrots, sliced
- 1 small onion, thinly sliced
- 1 small green bell pepper, cut into thin strips
- 1/2 cup vegetable oil
- 1/2 cup white sugar
- 1/4 cup distilled white vinegar
- 2 teaspoons almond extract
- 1 teaspoon dried basil

How to prepare:

- Boil carrots until tender but crisp. Remove from heat, drain, and place in a medium bowl with onion and pepper.
- In a medium saucepan over medium heat, blend oil, sugar, vinegar, almond extract and basil. Cook and stir until sugar is dissolved.
- Pour the oil mixture over the carrot mixture.

Cover, and chill in the refrigerator 8 hours or overnight before serving cold.

Nutritional facts:

Calories: 145kcal, Fat: 9.4g, Carbs: 15.4g, Protein: 0.7g, Sodium: 44mg

28. No Bake Granola Bars

Description:

Flaxseed is one of the richest plant-based sources of the anti-inflammatory omega-3 fatty acid ALA. Studies show it may help lower overall and LDL cholesterol and reduce the complications of diabetes and heart disease risk. Crushing or milling the flaxseed make it easier for your body to digest.

Ingredients:

- 2 cups rolled oats
- 1 1/4 cups natural crunchy peanut butter
- 1 cup ground flaxseed
- 3/4 cup honey
- 3/4 cup dried cranberries
- 1/2 cup chocolate chips
- 1/4 cup sliced almonds

How to prepare:

- Stir oats, peanut butter, flaxseed, honey, cranberries, chocolate chips, and almonds together in a bowl;
- Refrigerate mixture at least 1 hour.
- Cut into 12 bars and wrap each individually in

plastic wrap for storage.

Nutritional facts:

Calories: 391kcal, Fat: 21.3g, Carbs: 46.1g, Protein: 10.7g, Sodium: 136mg

29. Chia Seed Jam

Description:

Chia seeds are excellent source of anti-inflammatory, but their biggest benefit is probably their high fiber content. The fiber fills people up, which can help control weight.

Ingredients:

- 1/4 cup chia seeds
- 1/2 cup water
- 2 cups organic raspberries
- 1/2 cup organic blackberries
- 1/2 cup organic blueberries
- 2 organic strawberries, or more to taste
- 1/3 cup honey, or more to taste

How to prepare:

- Soak chia seeds in water until mixture has a jelly-like texture, about 5 minutes.
- Heat raspberries, blackberries, blueberries, strawberries, and honey in a saucepan over medium heat until berries are soft, about 15 minutes. Lightly crush berries with a fork or masher.
- Stir chia seed mixture into berry mixture. Remove

from heat and let cool for at least 10 minutes.

Nutritional facts:

Calories: 70kcal, Fat: 1g, Carbs: 15.3g, Protein: 1g, Sodium: 2mg

30. Sardine Salsa

Description:

A 3-ounce serving of sardines contains about 1.4 grams of omega-3 fats and is a good source of vitamin D, which helps our bodies absorb calcium to build and maintain strong bones.

Ingredients:

- 1 avocado, mashed
- 2 romaine lettuce leaves, chopped
- 1/4 green bell pepper, finely chopped
- 1 teaspoon lemon juice
- 4 slices French bread
- 2 teaspoons extra-virgin olive oil
- 1 (4.375 ounce) sardines, drained
- 1 (14.5 ounce) tomatoes with basil, garlic, and oregano - drained

How to prepare:

- Preheat oven to 350 degrees F (175 degrees C).
- Combine avocado, chopped lettuce, chopped green pepper, and lemon juice in a small bowl.
- Brush extra-virgin olive oil on bread slices and toast in the preheated oven until browned, about

5 minutes on each side.

Nutritional facts:

Calories: 275kcal, Fat: 14.1g, Carbs: 26g, Protein: 12.9g, Sodium: 920mg

31. Cali Smoothie

Description:

Instead of squeezing the juice of fruits and vegetables, you are putting whole items in – giving you the added bonus of fiber, which helps clean out arteries and fight constipation. Colorful fruits and vegetables are also high in antioxidants. Adding berries or leafy greens like spinach or kale can give you big doses of vitamins and nutrients.

Ingredients:

- 7 large strawberries
- 1 (8 ounce) container lemon yogurt
- 1/3 cup orange juice

How to prepare:

- Place strawberries in a plastic container and freeze for about an hour.
- In a blender, combine strawberries, yogurt and orange juice. Blend until smooth. Pour into a tall glass and serve.

Nutritional facts:

Calories: 281kcal, Fat: 0.9g, Carbs: 57.4g, Protein: 12.9g, Sodium: 155mg

32. Vitabombs

Description:

Green beans act as an easy source for acquiring vitamins like A, C, K, B6, and folic acid. In terms of minerals, green beans are a good source of calcium, silicon, iron, manganese, potassium, and copper.

Ingredients:

- 1 1/2 pounds green beans, trimmed and cut into 2 inch pieces
- 1 1/2 cups water
- 1 tablespoon olive oil
- 1 tablespoon sugar
- 3/4 teaspoon garlic salt
- 1/4 teaspoon pepper
- 1 1/2 teaspoons chopped fresh basil
- 2 cups cherry tomato halves

How to prepare:

- Place beans and water in a large saucepan. Cover, and bring to a boil. Set heat to low, and simmer until tender, about 10 minutes. Drain off water, and set aside.
- Stir in sugar, garlic salt, pepper and basil. Add

tomatoes, and cook stirring gently just until soft. Pour the tomato mixture over the green beans, and toss gently to blend.

Nutritional facts:

Calories: 122kcal, Fat: 8g, Carbs: 12.6g, Protein: 2.6g, Sodium: 294mg

33. Veggie-Stars

Description:

Beetroot is your everyday superfood. They are a pretty pink nutritional powerhouse and an excellent example of how food can work as medicine. They are rich in folic acid, iron, magnesium, manganese and phosphorus.

Ingredients:

- 250g cooked beetroot dipped in vinegar (not pickled)
- 1 tin butterbeans (410g), drained & rinsed
- 1-2 cloves garlic, crushed
- Small bunch fresh chives, finely chopped (reserve a few for garnish)
- 3tbsp extra virgin olive oil
- Sea salt & freshly ground black pepper

How to prepare:

- Chop the beetroot into small dice, set aside in a medium bowl.
- In a food processor blitz the butterbeans with the garlic, chives and olive oil. Season to taste with sea salt & freshly ground black pepper.

Nutritional facts:

Calories: 180kcal, Fat: 16g, Carbs: 6g, Protein: 3g, Sodium: 880mg

34. Garlicky Kale

Description:

Besides being crowned as the "queen of greens", kale could also be referred to as the queen of Vitamin A. Compared to any other leafy green vegetable, kale has over 100 per cent of the average person's daily Vitamin A and C requirement. Kale is often compared to oranges because of its richness in vitamins.

Ingredients:

- 1 bunch kale
- 2 tablespoons olive oil
- 4 cloves garlic, minced

How to prepare:

- Tear the kale leaves into bite-size pieces from the thick stems; discard the stems.
- Heat the olive oil in a large pot over medium heat. Cook and stir the garlic in the hot oil until softened, about 2 minutes.
- Add the kale and continue cooking and stirring until the kale is bright green and wilted, about 5 minutes more.

Nutritional facts:

Calories: 120kcal, Fat: 7.5g, Carbs: 12.2g, Protein: 3.9g, Sodium: 49mg

35. Primal Cauliflower Steaks

Description:

Add some color to your cauliflower with turmeric. Several recent studies show that turmeric has anti-inflammatory properties and modifies immune system responses. These cauliflower steaks are easy to prepare and would make an excellent vegetarian side or main dish.

Ingredients:

- 1 large (about 1.2kg) cauliflower
- 1/4 cup extra virgin olive oil, plus extra for frying
- 1 teaspoon ground turmeric
- Fried curry leaves, to serve
- Thinly sliced fried red chilli, to serve

How to prepare:

- Preheat oven to 340F fan forced. Line 2 baking trays with foil.
- Cut the cauliflower into four 1.5cm-thick slices, leaving base intact. Cook steaks in extra virgin olive oil for 2-3 minutes each side or until golden.
- Whisk the olive oil with the turmeric in a bowl until combined. Brush over steaks.
- Roast cauliflower in the oven for 12-15 minutes or

until tender and crisp.

Nutritional facts:

Calories: 161kcal, Fat: 15g, Carbs: 7g, Protein: 2.4g, Sodium: 30.8mg

36. Olive Dip

Description:

Though technically a fruit and not found in the produce aisle, olives and olive oil can be potent inflammation fighters. Olive contains compounds with anti-inflammatory properties. These compounds can dampen or switch off 100 inflammation causing genes.

Ingredients:

- 1 (4 ounce) can chopped green chiles, drained
- 1 onion, chopped
- 1 (5 ounce) jar green olives, chopped (reserve brine)
- 1 (6 ounce) can chopped black olives
- 1 1/2 cups shredded Cheddar cheese
- ground black pepper to taste
- garlic salt to taste
- 2 fresh red tomatoes, chopped

How to prepare:

- Chill a serving bowl in the freezer while you make the salsa.
- In a mixing bowl, combine the chopped green chiles, onion, green olives, and black olives.

- Lightly mix in the Cheddar cheese and tomatoes; season to taste with garlic salt and black pepper. If desired, mix in a little bit of the olive brine.
- Serve in the chilled bowl.

Nutritional facts:

Calories: 42kcal, Fat: 3.2g, Carbs: 1.9g, Protein: 1.8g, Sodium: 253mg

37. Round Veggie Chips

Description:

Oven-fried zucchini chips taste like they're fried, yet they are baked and amazingly crispy. These chips make a healthy substitute for french fries. Zucchini is rich in Vitamins A and C as well as antioxidants.

Ingredients:

- 3 small zucchini, sliced into ¼- inch rounds
- 2 tablespoons olive oil
- ½ cup Italian seasoned bread crumbs
- 2 tablespoons grated Parmesan cheese
- 2 teaspoons fresh oregano

How to prepare:

- Preheat oven to 350 degrees F (175 degrees C).
- Place zucchini in a bowl. Drizzle olive oil over zucchini and stir to coat; add bread crumbs and toss to coat. Spread coated zucchini onto a baking sheet. Sprinkle Parmesan cheese and oregano over coated zucchini.
- Bake in the preheated oven until zucchini are tender and cheese is browned, about 15 minutes

Nutritional facts:

Calories: 92kcal, Fat: 2g, Carbs: 14g, Protein: 6g, Sodium: 340mg

38. Kung-Fu Watercress

Description:

Iron is important in preventing anaemia and many people with arthritis are anaemic. Watercress is one of good sources of iron.

Ingredients:

- 1/2 cup chopped dried cranberries
- 1/4 cup red wine vinegar
- 1/4 cup balsamic vinegar
- 1 tablespoon minced garlic
- 1 1/4 teaspoons salt
- 1 cup extra virgin olive oil
- 6 bunches watercress - rinsed, dried and trimmed
- 3 bulbs fennel - trimmed, cored and thinly sliced
- 3 small heads radicchio, cored and chopped
- 1 cup pecan halves, toasted

How to prepare:

- In a bowl, combine the cranberries, red wine vinegar, balsamic vinegar, garlic and salt. Whisk in the olive oil.
- In a large salad bowl, combine the watercress, fennel, radicchio and pecans. Stir the vinaigrette

and pour over salad. Toss well and serve at once.

Nutritional facts:

Calories: 178kcal, Fat: 15.4g, Carbs: 8.9g, Protein: 3.1g, Sodium: 202mg

39. OMG Oat

Description:

Omega-3 fatty acids are a key ingredient in helping to reduce the inflammation of arthritis and other joint problems, but getting enough of it every day can be challenging. This oatmeal tastes great and gets you half your daily requirements of omega-3s.

Ingredients:

- 1 cup rolled organic oats
- 1 cup filtered water
- 2 tbsp acidic medium (yogurt, lemon juice, apple cider vinegar, buttermilk)
- ½ tsp unrefined sea salt

How to prepare:

- Add 1 cup of oats, water, and the acidic medium into a glass bowl and stir well. Cover and let it sit overnight on the counter (at least 7-8 hours).
- In the morning add another 1 cup of filtered water and the unrefined sea salt, stir well.
- Heat to a low simmer and cook for 5 minutes.
- Serve with a generous portion of butter and cream.

Nutritional facts:

Calories: 153kcal, Fat: 3g, Carbs: 28.3g, Protein: 5.1g, Sodium: 202mg

40. Coconut Pumpkin Bread

Description:

Pumpkins are an excellent source of beta-cryptoxanthin, a powerful anti-inflammatory. This antioxidant is absorbed best when paired with a fat. Pumpkin skins are edible which makes preparing this bread very easy!

Ingredients:

- 4 eggs
- 3/4 cup canned organic pumpkin
- 1/4 cup coconut oil (melted and cooled)
- 1 tbsp raw honey
- 1/2 tsp unrefined sea salt
- 1/4 tsp baking soda
- 3/4 cup coconut flour
- 1 tsp cinnamon
- 1 tsp pumpkin spice

How to prepare:

- Blend together wet **Ingredients:** eggs, pumpkin, cooled coconut oil, honey and mix well.
- In another bowl combine dry **Ingredients:** salt, baking soda, coconut flour, cinnamon, pumpkin spice and shredded coconut.

- Combine wet and dry ingredients and stir until their are no more lumps.
- Pour into a greased bread pan and bake on 350 F for 40-45 minutes.

Nutritional facts:

Calories: 225.3kcal, Fat: 14g, Carbs: 14.4g, Protein: 7.3g

41. Raspberry Smoothie

Description:

Looking for a quick and easy breakfast which full of vitamin C? Try a smoothie. You can make this ahead of time and store it in the fridge. Just grab it and go before you head out the door. For lower sugar intake, use unsweetened yogurt.

Ingredients:

- 350g fresh raspberries
- 1 cup fresh strawberries, hulled, roughly chopped
- 1 1/2 cups (about 180g) natural yoghurt
- 1 cup milk

How to prepare:

- Place strawberries, raspberries, yoghurt, and milk in a blender. Blend until smooth. Pour into glasses. Serve.

Nutritional facts:

Calories: 160.3kcal, Fat: 4g, Carbs: 22g, Protein: 6g, Sodium: 65.83mg

42. Ginger's Secrets

Description:

Not only does ginger taste great in these quick and easy beverage, but it's also an excellent anti-inflammatory, helping to ease arthritis pain.

Ingredients:

- 1 cup chilled orange juice
- 1 cup chilled apple juice
- 2 tablespoons ginger beer cordial
- 1 tablespoon chopped fresh mint leaves
- 4 strawberries, hulled, roughly chopped
- 2 cups chilled lemonade
- ice cubes, to serve

How to prepare:

- Combine orange juice, apple juice and cordial in a large bowl. Top with mint, strawberries, lemonade and ice. Stir to combine. Serve.

Nutritional facts:

Calories: 95kcal, Carbs: 22g, Protein: 1g, Sodium: 28.3mg

43. Cranberry Sauce

Description:

Cranberry juice is able to block this bacteria from growing and multiplying; researchers believe that patients in the early stages of rheumatoid arthritis can benefit from a high intake of cranberry juice.

Ingredients:

- 12 ounces cranberries
- 1 cup white sugar
- 1 cup orange juice

How to prepare:

- In a medium sized saucepan over medium heat, dissolve the sugar in the orange juice. Stir in the cranberries and cook until the cranberries start to pop (about 10 minutes). Remove from heat and place sauce in a bowl. Cranberry sauce will thicken as it cools.

Nutritional facts:

Calories : 95kcal, Fat : 14g, Carbs : 24g, Protein : 7.3g

44. Honey Yummy Pineapple

Description:

Pineapple contains immune-boosting vitamin C. It also provides a key enzyme called bromelain, which is chock-full of anti-inflammatory substances that can help reduce joint swelling linked to rheumatoid arthritis.

Ingredients:

- 4 slices fresh pineapple
- 2 tablespoons honey
- 1 teaspoon lemon juice

How to prepare:

- To Marinate: Combine honey, brandy and lemon juice in a nonporous glass dish or bowl. Mix together and add pineapple; coat well with marinade mixture. Cover dish and marinate in refrigerator for 1 hour.
- Preheat grill to medium heat and lightly oil grate.
- Remove pineapple from dish or bowl, discarding any leftover marinade. Place pineapple wedges directly on rack or in a basket and grill for about 10 minutes, turning, until pineapple is hot and caramelized.

Nutritional facts:

Calories : 59kcal, Fat : 0.1, Carbs : 11.8g, Protein : 0.3g

45. Senor Pineapple

Description:

Pineapple is rich in magnesium, manganese and a vital enzyme known as bromelain. It also contains copper, potassium, vitamin B1, vitamin B6, dietary fibre, folate and pantothenic acid.

Ingredients:

- 1 cup brown sugar
- 2 teaspoons ground cinnamon
- 1 pineapple - peeled, cored, and cut into 6 wedges

How to prepare:

- Preheat an outdoor grill for medium-high heat and lightly oil the grate.
- Whisk brown sugar and cinnamon together in a bowl. Pour sugar mixture into a large resealable plastic bag. Place pineapple wedges in bag and shake to coat each wedge.
- Grill pineapple wedges on the preheated grill until heated through, 3 to 5 minutes per side.

Nutritional facts:

Calories: 225kcal, Fat: 0.3g, Carbs: 66g, Protein: 1.3g,

Sodium: 13mg

46. Dinner Bass

Description:

Eating more than one serving of all types of fish every week for a minimum of 10 years will reduce the risk of arthritis by 29%!

Ingredients:

- 1 lemon, juiced
- 3 tablespoons olive oil
- 2 tablespoons chopped fresh parsley
- 1 pinch crushed red pepper flakes
- 1 pinch salt
- 1 pound skinless wild striped bass fillets

How to prepare:

- Whisk together lemon juice, olive oil, parsley, pepper flakes, and salt in a bowl. Add bass fillets; marinate for 10 minutes.
- Preheat an outdoor grill for medium-high heat and lightly oil the grate.
- Grill bass on the preheated grill until fish flakes easily with a fork, about 5 minutes each side. Discard any remaining marinade.

Nutritional facts:

Calories: 226kcal, Fat: 15.5g, Carbs: 3.1g, Protein: 21.8g, Sodium: 179mg

47. Legacy of Pear

Description:

One pear contains up to 11 percent of our daily recommended intake of vitamin C and 9.5 percent of our daily recommended intake of copper. Pears are also said to have more nutrients per calorie than calorie per nutrient.

Ingredients:

- 1 ripe pear - peeled, cored, and chopped
- 1/2 cup white wine
- 1 clove garlic, chopped
- 2 teaspoons Dijon mustard
- 1/4 cup white balsamic vinegar
- 1 teaspoon ground black pepper
- 1/4 teaspoon sea salt
- 1/2 cup olive oil

How to prepare:

- Blend the pear, white wine, garlic, Dijon mustard, white balsamic vinegar, black pepper, and sea salt in a blender until well combined; drizzle the olive oil into the mixture in a thin, steady stream while continuing to blend. Blend a few seconds longer until the salad dressing is thick and creamy.

Nutritional facts:

Calories: 101kcal, Fat: 9g, Carbs: 3.6g, Protein: 0.1g, Sodium: 60mg

48. Japanese pickled ginger

Description:

Do you keep ginger in your spice cabinet? Maybe it should be in your medicine cabinet. Besides being a tasty spice often used to enhance holiday treats, ginger can soothe upset stomachs and diminish nausea, and studies show it may help pain and inflammation, too.

Ingredients:

- 125g fresh ginger, peeled
- 1 teaspoon salt
- 60ml (1/4 cup) rice wine vinegar
- 60ml (1/4 cup) water
- 55g (1/4 cup) caster sugar

How to prepare:

- Slice the ginger into thin strips. Transfer to a bowl and sprinkle with salt. Stir until well combined. Set aside for 30 minutes to allow the salt to extract excess liquid.
- Stir the rice wine vinegar, water and sugar in a small saucepan over medium heat until the sugar dissolves. Increase heat to high. Bring to the boil. Pour the vinegar mixture over ginger. Set aside for

5 minutes to cool slightly. Seal and place in the fridge for 24 hours to develop the flavours.

Nutritional facts:

Calories: 16kcal, Carbs :3.5g

49. Sparkle of Watermelon & Ginger

Description:

The anti-inflammatory properties help relieve pain and improve function for all types of arthritis. Mix ginger and watermelon together and make a good use of them.

Ingredients:

- 1kg piece seedless watermelon, skin removed, cut into chunks
- 2 cups ice cubes
- 1/4 cup fresh mint leaves
- 2 tablespoons caster sugar
- 1 teaspoon finely grated fresh ginger

How to prepare:

- Place watermelon in a blender. Blend until finely chopped. Add ice, mint leaves, sugar and ginger. Blend until ice is crushed.
- Pour into serving glasses and serve immediately.

Nutritional facts:

Calories: 114kcal, Fat: 1g, Carbs: 24g, Protein: 1g, Sodium: 5.31mg

50. Pickled Onion

Description:

Onions are low in calories, have virtually no fat and are loaded with healthful components that fight inflammation in arthritis and related conditions. One flavonoid found in onions, called quercetin, has been shown to inhibit inflammation.

Ingredients:

- 1 red onion, chopped
- 1/2 cup red wine vinegar
- 3 tablespoons distilled white vinegar
- 1 1/2 tablespoons salt
- 1 teaspoons white sugar

How to prepare:

- Bring the onion, red wine vinegar, white vinegar, salt, and sugar to a boil in a saucepan over medium-high heat. Remove from heat and allow mixture to steep until the onion is tender, about 20 minutes.

Nutritional facts:

Calories: 19kcal, Fat: 0g, Carbs: 4.5g, Protein: 0.2g,

Sodium: 1745mg

51. Two-tone Granitas

Description:

How to make a cool dessert in the hot summer and be healthy with your arthritis pain? Let's beat the heat and pain with this sweet grape granita.

Ingredients:

- 500g red grapes, picked
- 500g green grapes, picked
- 750ml (3 cups) water
- 270g (1/4 cups) caster sugar

How to prepare:

- Place the red grapes in the jug of a blender and blend until pureed. Pour through a fine sieve into a medium bowl, gently pressing with the back of a spoon to extract as much liquid as possible. Discard the skins and seeds. Repeat with green grapes.
- Combine the water and sugar in a saucepan over low heat. Cook, stirring, for 2-3 minutes or until sugar dissolves. Increase heat to medium-high and bring to a simmer. Simmer for 8-10 minutes or until syrup thickens slightly. Remove from heat

and set aside for 10 minutes to cool.
- Add half the sugar mixture to the red grape juice and remaining sugar mixture to green grape juice. Pour into separate airtight containers and cover with lids. Place in the freezer for 3-4 hours or until ice crystals form around the edges. Use a fork to roughly break up the frozen grape juice. Cover and return to the freezer for a further 8 hours or until completely set.
- Use a fork to scrape the granitas into coarse crystals. Cover and return to the freezer for a further 1 hour.
- Divide the red grape granita and green grape granita among serving glasses and serve immediately.

Nutritional facts:

Calories: 455kcal, Carbs: 107g, Protein: 2g, Sodium: 10.5mg

52. Kiwi Cooler

Description:

Research suggests that people who eat a diet low in vitamin C may have a greater risk of developing some kinds of arthritis. Kiwi is one of vitamin C-rich foods!

Ingredients:

- 1/2 cup (110g) caster sugar
- 1/2 cup (125ml) boiling water
- 4 gold and 4 green kiwi fruit
- 1/3 cup (80ml) lime juice (from 3-4 limes)
- 1/2 cup mint leaves
- 2 cups ice cubes
- 1 cup (250ml) sparkling water

How to prepare:

- In a large jug, dissolve 1/2 cup (110g) caster sugar in 1/2 cup (125ml) boiling water, then place in an ice bath or fridge to chill. Peel and roughly chop 4 gold and 4 green kiwi fruit, then blend until smooth with the cooled syrup, 1/3 cup (80ml) lime juice, 1/2 firmly packed cup mint leaves and 2 cups ice cubes. Pour into a jug and top up with 1 cup (250ml) sparkling water, or divide among glasses and top up with wine or water. Serve with extra mint.

Nutritional facts:

Calories: 92kcal, Carbs: 18g, Protein: 1g, Sodium: 9.6mg

53. Kiwifruit Break

Description:

Eat some kiwi and get vitamin C in your breakfast. Time to start a new day!

Ingredients:

- 4 kiwifruit, peeled, chopped
- 1 red capsicum, halved, seeded, cut into 1cm pieces
- 2 shallots, ends trimmed, thinly sliced
- 1/3 cup fresh coriander, chopped
- 2 teaspoons fresh lime juice

How to prepare:

- Place the kiwifruit, capsicum, shallot, coriander and lime juice in a glass or ceramic bowl. Season with salt and pepper. Stir gently until well combined.

Nutritional facts:

Calories: 56kcal, Fat: 0.5g, Carbs: 11g, Protein: 2g

ADDITIONAL TITLES FROM THIS AUTHOR

70 Effective Meal Recipes to Prevent and Solve Being Overweight: Burn Fat Fast by Using Proper Dieting and Smart Nutrition

By

Joe Correa CSN

48 Acne Solving Meal Recipes: The Fast and Natural Path to Fixing Your Acne Problems in Less Than 10 Days!

By

Joe Correa CSN

41 Alzheimer's Preventing Meal Recipes: Reduce or Eliminate Your Alzheimer's Condition in 30 Days or Less!

By

Joe Correa CSN

70 Effective Breast Cancer Meal Recipes: Prevent and Fight Breast Cancer with Smart Nutrition and Powerful Foods

By

Joe Correa CSN

www.ingramcontent.com/pod-product-compliance
Lightning Source LLC
Chambersburg PA
CBHW052015070526
44584CB00016B/1767